Books by Steve Erickson

LEAP

YEAR

Steve Erickson

POSEIDON PRESS

New York London Toronto Sydney Tokyo

POSEIDON PRESS
Simon & Schuster Building
Rockefeller Center
1230 Avenue of the Americas
New York, New York 10020

POSEIDON PRESS is a registered trademark
of Simon & Schuster Inc.

POSEIDON PRESS colophon is a trademark
of Simon & Schuster Inc.

Designed by Beth Tondreau Design / Jane Treuhaft
Manufactured in the United States of America

10 9 8 7 6 5 4 3 2 1

LIBRARY OF CONGRESS CATALOGING-IN-PUBLICATION DATA
Erickson, Steve.
  Leap year / Steve Erickson.
  p.   cm.
  1. Presidents—United States—Election—1988. 2. United States—
Politics and government—1981–1989. 3. Erickson, Steve—Journeys—
United States. I. Title.
E880E75 1989
324.973'0927—dc20   89-35383
                                                         CIP

ISBN 0-671-67134-0

And when you reach the broken promise land
Every dream slips through your hands
And you know it's too late to change your mind

—*Freddie Fender*

Sally speaks to me. *I can't live with the things you feel* she says *it's enough to live with the things I feel. It's enough to live with the feeling of the country flowing through me. Don't tell me you expect nothing of me because I won't believe you. Don't tell me you ask nothing of me because I hear the unspoken questions in the rush of your breath when I first speak to you.* She's right about this, something happens to my breathing when I hear her, though the way it changes is not necessarily guilty of anything. *I'm guilty of too many things* she says as though reading my mind *I can't be responsible for you too. Go home. I've been looking for Thomas.* But I remember how she called me Thomas, the first time I saw her.

• • •

This morning Josef brings the doors. The old doors of our apartment are curling at the bottom; beneath them the night blows in dead moths, sawdust, the fumes of Filipino stew from the house next door. Josef, the building's handyman, comes from Poland, where a murky affiliation with Solidarity kept him in and out of jails six years, until he fled leaving his family behind. Now a husky blond woman accompanies him. He brings new doors from a doorstore, or an industry of doors perhaps: the first ones don't fit. They're too small. He leaves, comes back an hour later with larger doors that are a shade too large and must be shaved along the edges. Josef is taciturn and haunted, unhappy; his handiwork is earnest but raw. He makes a mess but means well; it's his sawdust from other labors I must assume has blown in beneath the old curled doors that were on these same hinges hours ago. Tomorrow when Josef goes to fix the neighbor's doors, the neighbor will chase him away, verbally abusing him in a way he never heard even in Poland; even the Communist authorities didn't speak to him this way. . . .

Tonight it's the twenty-eighth of February, 1988, an hour and a half short of Leap Year's extra number. Where the extra day itself falls remains unknown to me; I'm keeping an eye out for it. Everything's been electric lately. Lately everything I touch gives off an electric shock: doorknobs, the railing of stairs, the water from the faucet, the car when I get out. I put my finger to the object, raise it to my lips: electricity. I slap things first to ground myself. I assault the metal around me on a constant basis, before it can strike me back. The keys on my ring hum with voltage; I must grab them with my teeth clenched, before dropping them in my pocket where they might ignite a naked nerve. My day's filled with hitting things. Only at night, on a mattress that holds no current, do I confront a different electricity altogether.

Maybe the extra day has already come and gone, with ramifications not yet felt. Maybe, by the sheerest coincidence, it will fall tomorrow, in correspondence with the number designed for it.

The problem isn't with the doors. It's with the doorways. The earthquakes of recent days have shifted all the doorways in this building, the street, the neighborhood, I suppose, until the old doors curl at the bottom and the new doors don't fit. For three hours Josef shaves the new door on the sides until it fits at the top, and is now too small at the bottom. A huge gap of daylight shines through the bottom from the outside. Half of America could blow through. Convulsed eagles and the desperate stench of the homeless. This afternoon my wife spoke to a friend whose husband works in the San Fernando Valley for NASA: they've been measuring the movements of the earth the last six months. The wife of the man who works for NASA relays inside information to the effect that the earth is moving in precognitive fashion, along the buckled temporal fault lines of Leap Year; the conviction of experts at NASA has it that the cataclysmic quake of legend and prophecy is likelier to happen this year than any other. Astrid's friend says, I don't want to scare you. She says NASA is shipping her husband food and supplies in secret for the pending disaster. There's no reason to expect that this quake, depending when it should hit, won't kill many thousands of people and level the city for months; its residents will live a quasiprehistoric existence, traveling by foot on undrivable roads, bartering goods in the absence of functioning bank computers, fleeing the fires that roar from the earth and then returning to hover around them on cold unsheltered nights. Safe at night on my currentless mattress from the electricity of life around me, I sleep my way toward the explosion of terra roulette; it could as easily be tomorrow morning as any other. On the extra day of Leap Year, when time collapses into a hole, the earth may as well. . . .

America, which against every denial it might muster both longs for and despises the future that Los Angeles means, will sort through that future's rubble like a seer through leaves of tea. I take this warning of my wife's friend's husband seriously, because it's Leap Year. Because America and whatever function it's determined to perform in the evolution of moral time will insist on reducing its future to a physical rubble if only to be free of it once and for all. It's a future still waiting to understand the past is dead: an America that waits to understand it's now only the United States. Sometime next year, close to the two hundredth anniversary of the first inauguration of America's first president, someone will become the leader of a country that no longer is.

Has this ever happened before? It's no wonder that those contending for the distinction are strangers: an election of strangers—ten men at this particular moment, plus half a dozen occasionally mentioned as alternatives to any of the ten. Of these sixteen the odds are high that a year from now the president of the United States will have one of five names: Bush, Dole, Dukakis, Gephardt, or Cuomo, the most familiar of whom, the current vice president, has by all appearances no political identity whatsoever. If, when you read this, the above statement has not been borne out, it will only be a mark of how strange this year has become after all. If the future has indeed had its geological brains splattered across the landscape in the fiery crack of terra roulette, and some of us are gone, then read what's here as drool from the dark of the year's abysmal day, where time is seen coming and going.

• • •

We live in the MacArthur Park section of Los Angeles, about five minutes west of Downtown and about ten minutes east of Hollywood. It's an interesting section of town. There are many poor people, most of them latino, as well as students from the art institute, businesspeople from Wilshire Boulevard three blocks away, and black yuppies who live just off Lafayette Park. I've lived in this apartment ten years. It's shocking to realize I've lived in this apartment longer than in any other residence of my life, including the houses of my childhood. I've lived here indeed longer than in all the other residences of my adulthood combined, scattered as they were between the time I was eighteen and twenty-eight, when I moved in here. I lived most of this time alone; Astrid moved in two and a half years ago and we got married six months after that. It's a charming apartment, divided into upstairs and down, which sometimes provides the illusion it's bigger than it is. It's not very big at all. There's something to be said for this, it necessitates owning a minimum of stuff. It imposes a sort of quality-control process on my records, which simply must fit into one corner of the apartment, and my books, which simply must fit against one wall. When the corner's filled up, when the wall's filled up, records go, books go. Nothing's immune, there's no room for sentiment for the earnest admirable effort that doesn't become indispensable to keep. Bob Dylan is not immune. Van Morrison, my favorite musician of all time, is not immune. All right, my Mott the Hoople records are immune. William Faulkner's immune. Henry Miller and Miles Davis are *almost* immune. My twenty-record box set of Frank Sinatra, a nuisance of a thing that takes up whole *inches*, is immune. . . .

For a while I didn't have anything more to say. I was working in a comic-book store on Melrose Avenue. This is the main drag of Pop Angeles; it used to be art galleries and thrift shops, and then about a decade ago punk seized control of its low-rent aspects. Now there are retro diners and record stores and gelato shops and trendy eateries and this comic-book store where I worked. Punks and New Hollywood moguls and alleged bohemians and tourists and counterculture newspaper editors from Oregon who can't wait to move to New York because Los Angeles isn't hip enough for them all collide on Melrose Avenue; a Jewish retirement home sits in the middle of it; Holocaust victims on the patio watch the passing parade. I worked in the comic-book store about eight months. I attended to the needs of adolescent boys who required this issue or that of *Punisher* or *Teenage Mutant Ninja Turtles*. I also had to put up with the grownups, young men in suits and ties who would burst in red-faced and hot under the collar about the way Superman was stripped of certain facets of his X-ray vision in the most recent adventure. The most appealing thing about the job was the way everyone thought it was beneath me. Even the other people who worked at the store thought it was beneath me, though not necessarily beneath them. This was just something I had to overcome, it just took time to persuade people that it wasn't beneath me at all, that I was in fact perfectly suited to such an occupation. By the end of the time I worked there they believed this. I completely convinced them. I left finally because there was something to say again, and so I wrote another book and now that's over and it's the beginning of another year. It's still early in the year, the year's still crisp and unslept in, when I know I'm going to leave Los Angeles for a while.

• • •

It's not because of the coming earthquake. Truth is, it's the coming earthquake that almost keeps me here. It's what's happening in the rest of the country, it's the cataclysm out there that I rush to be a part of. I try to carefully explain this to Astrid. I explain she may join me at whatever point of time and place in the journey she chooses. She knows though I'll do this alone. She knows she'll stay here with the curling doors and feed our cats and give the asthmatic one who snorted and sniveled his way into our lives his medicine at night. Nothing's definite about why or how long I may be gone. It's deeper than mere restlessness. For weeks I postpone the departure, the suitcase sits on the top shelf of the closet until mere hours before my train leaves.

• • •

I'm not looking for America. It's not that. Enough people over enough years have done that, they looked as far as the sun illuminated their line of vision, until they couldn't follow that light any further. I'm going against the light. I'll take the spare twenty-four hours of sun the year offers; I may find it in Missouri. I may find it in Albuquerque. At eight-thirty on a Sunday night my suitcase is down from the top shelf of the closet; I'm in Union Station in Los Angeles. The train hums and shudders for departure: I have my own compartment, two seats that make a bed, curtains on the window that don't quite reach edge to edge.

The attendant is handing out menus down the aisle; the dining car is the one next to mine. When I'm done this trip will take me by train and auto seven thousand miles across twenty-three states. Navigations of the map will be as circular as the shadow around a sundial; itineraries will be spliced and reassembled. I'll travel as though to throw someone off my trail. Any one of many hours may be Leap Year's random twenty-four. . . .

• • •

I'm advised in the little booklet they give me on the train that one of the highlights of my trip is the birthplace of Walt Disney. Several people who have taken this train before have said the same thing to me over the last couple of weeks. "Oh yes, you'll go right through the birthplace of Walt Disney." In fact the clever strategists of the train company have arranged the schedule in such a fashion that one pretty much wakes up to the birthplace of Walt Disney, having slept through Kansas. I have to believe this is part of the plan too, the sleeping through Kansas, the train hitting dark around Colorado and daylight again on the Missouri side of St. Louis. There's just nothing anyone can do with Kansas, its flat desolation holding appeal only for weird antisocial passengers who stay in their compartments. I'm fixed to my compartment, except for occasions in New Mexico when it doesn't seem too early to head for the lounge car. The major and somewhat disconcerting task of my days on the train is pondering, and reaching some decision on, whether today I'm going to go with bourbon or vodka, since one of the emerging characteristics of my maturation is a strict adherence to either one or the other over a twenty-four-hour period of time. Amerindian guides help those of us in the lounge car over the rough spots of New Mexico, given that it's almost impossible to believe, without expert verification, that the earth turns that red that quickly after crossing the border.

Thus, hanging out in the lounge car and then the dining

car, I can't help but talk to this person or that. Most of the
conversations have to do with the train itself; everyone's first
assumption is that everyone else on the train is afraid of airplanes,
though in fact this seems never to be the case. This is around the
time that various airplanes here and there are dissolving in
midair, the roof flying off or whatever. But no one can understand
why anyone else would take the train otherwise, if it isn't from a
fear of airplanes. The romanticism of the train is presumed too
precious or idiotic for anyone else to share it. I explain that I took
many trains when I lived in Europe and wanted to take one here.
Invariably and dreadfully we get around to this book. People
don't speak of any of the five people who seem to me likely to be
elected president eight months from now, always they talk about
the man who will not be elected. They never talk about the fact
he's a black man. Maybe they care about this and maybe they
don't. They don't say, "Now, I don't care whether he's black or
not." It must say something about the country that we've either
grown cagier about our racism or it at least has become a side
issue. Not everyone is enthusiastic about him but it seems
completely understood that he represents something important
beyond the consequences of November, or even beyond the
consequences of the four years to follow. "I think he's got a lot of
good ideas," a white woman from Reseda says to me. "But I don't
like this business of him going off to this country or that with
Castro or Arafat. He had no business doing that." I believe her.
I think this may be what genuinely bothers her about him. I sense
from several people feelings about the man both good and bad
that are more than euphemisms for something else. Only later
will it be unsettling to learn, from people who have a great deal
of experience riding trains, that people who ride trains in this
country are liars. They may not be liars before boarding the train
but they become liars the moment they're out of the station, or
maybe even before they've left the station, and in fact one of the
principal reasons people take trains is so they can lie their heads

off about everything, their pasts and destinations, and whatever reasons link the two. People will cheerfully admit how they get on the train and lie to everyone they meet about everything, creating panoplies of lives and personae; it's one of the fringe benefits of train riding. So who's to tell what's true of what anyone says about people running for president who lie for a living, which is to say people who have a great deal in common with myself. . . .

My first night I sleep with my head pointed toward the front of the train. The bed unfolds parallel with the window. When I'm sleeping with my head pointed toward the front of the train, I feel as though I'm being pulled further and further into the country by my dreams. I'm being pulled against the light by my own eyes, and when I shut my eyes it's like falling head first down a tunnel in a bodylong tube. It's an interesting way to travel but I don't sleep worth a damn. It's a sign of age or cowardice that I'm not willing to sacrifice the peace for the revelation. The next morning I wake outside Flagstaff and read in the newspaper about people in the West who are now renting fake car phones in order that they may ride around in their cars on the freeways or highways or along the streets impressing people in other cars by speaking into car phones that don't work. All through the Southwest I see them, whisking by on the interstates that run alongside the train, people in their cars having conversations with no one on telephones that connect to nothing. It's possible, however, that unlike the people on trains, such conversationalists tell the truth.

• • •

I was born in America; it was somewhere inland. My father was the son of immigrants from Stockholm, my mother the descendant of French settlers and American Indians. One sees little of the Indian in my mother and none in me, but in a scrapbook at my parents' home there's a picture of my grandfather who died before I was born, and one definitely sees the Indian in him. Dark and angular in his facial structure, a bit of Asia around the eyes. I still receive with some frequency a newsletter from my tribe in Oklahoma. When I was a toddler thirty-five years ago living on the southern edge of the San Fernando Valley, there was one phone line in Encino. By the time I was six and the lines had been laid, my family moved north with tens of thousands of others, electricity and communication slithering ahead beneath our feet to the other edge of the valley where there was nothing but ranches and orchards and fields and horses thundering through the gullies, and loud dogs on the hillsides, at a time when the nights of the valley still had voids and the long plains of dirt and dust were just becoming studded with the new emblem of victoryflushed America, the tract house. The nuclear age built the valley. The exploration of outer space built the valley. I grew up and it changed. It changed in *days*. After seven years we moved from the tract house, the plains of dirt and dust having given way to lawns and pools. A decade after the dirt and dust gave way to lawns and pools, a freeway was built and the lawns and pools gave way again to dirt and dust, the neighborhood of my childhood having lived its entire life within the time of that childhood. I left home. I left the country for a while. I went to Paris and New York where, when the earth moves beneath your feet, it's a train. I came home to Los Angeles where, when the earth moves beneath your feet, it's the earth. I went back to see the house where I grew up, they were still building the freeway. The house was gone but our swimming pool was still there, having missed the boundary line of the bulldozers and been given by the county to our former next-door neighbors whose house also remained. Thus beneath the beams of an unfinished freeway disappearing in the dark above new moonscapes of dirt and dust what was left of my childhood was a lone patch of blue shimmering in the twilight, claimed by the appendage of chainlink fence that jutted hungrily into the wasteland from our neighbors' yard. Six years ago I reconciled myself to living in temporary residence on a hill above the Disposable City near the city's nonexistent center.

Not far from where I live is where the huge walls of Griffith's *Intolerance* once stood, now replaced by a Von's market; on the stretch of Sunset Boulevard that runs past it is a billboard from the Virgin Mary. "The Virgin Mary has a message for America," it reads, "call TODAY. 888-1111." I picture the Virgin's switchboard jammed with calls from all those car telephones that don't call anywhere. At about the same distance in the other direction is Broadway, the eastern edge of the city beyond which one ceases even to imagine a city, unless one lives in that part of the city in which case Broadway is the western edge where everything begins. It's ten blocks of dinful Spanish chatter seething with wedding shops and shoe stores and magazine stands with *La Opinion* and the black *Los Angeles Sentinel*, movie houses with posters for films like *Rosa de la Frontera* about vigilante Mexican women with shotguns, and an occasional Chuck Norris picture from the United States. There is a rumor on Broadway that the United States is in close proximity. Newspaper reporters from the *Los Angeles Times*, models from the fashion mart, albino bums from Pershing Square, black men selling makeup kits and Chicanas selling umbrellas that hang from their arms under an utterly cloudless sky, construction workers carrying a single red rose to their girlfriends who work the orange-juice stand up near Fifth, all surge up and down Broadway shopping, eating, considering marriage, darting into doorways that open onto huge marketplaces with fresh dead meat and the China Café downstairs and shelves of tequila rising twenty feet high, Clifton's cafeteria with plaster rock formations inside and waterfalls and slides of forests projected on the walls, the vertiginous spiraling Bradbury Building of cast iron and tile and a skylight hovering five stories overhead built in the last two decades of the Nineteenth Century by a mining executive who got the idea for it from a science fiction story and contracted an architect who refused to build it until he got the approval of his dead brother through a Ouija board.

A third of the people who live in East Los Angeles, according to the City of Los Angeles and the United States of America, do not exist. They live on the other side of the Los Angeles River, which nobody can find and which runs from no point of origin that can be determined but which, according to the City of Los Angeles and maps of the environs, does exist. Go south on Broadway several miles and you come to Watts. Twenty-three years ago when the Watts riots took place, people in my neighborhood in the valley thirty miles away talked about arming themselves. They were going to fight it out with the Other Los Angeles when it came streaming over the Cahuenga Pass; as it happened the Other Los Angeles never got to the Cahuenga Pass, its only casualties being thirty-four of its own.

One night, about ten into the new year, I sat with two friends in an old Hollywood bar called Boardner's; a couple of us were married and the other had been. It was about one-thirty in the morning. A certain amount of vodka inspired my compatriots to blithely, almost cheerfully, predict that my worst fears must invariably come true. It was the sort of night to the memory of which one wakes the next morning appalled at what he's revealed, not so much to others but to himself. Boardner's has red booths and photos on the wall and a jukebox that tries to be modern even as everyone keeps punching Bunny Berigan songs. The people there are pleasant enough usually but you can't imagine where they go when they leave, particularly since the only car parked on the dark, grim little street outside is yours. The obvious thought is that they don't leave. When did these people come here? When did they know Los Angeles wasn't going to make them into the people they thought they could be? When did they stop counting all the corners of the city around which they thought they could lose themselves? Where for them did the West stop moving east, how many Other Los Angeleses translate a ludicrous dream into a best hope, then a best hope into a small one, then a small one into a mean resignation, then a mean resignation into a night at Boardner's? Last time I was there some years ago a friend of mine pulled out a water pistol and shot a guy. It was funny at the time but not so especially smart. The guy she shot was in his late forties, a block of a guy in a dark coat and a dark shirt with his hair cut close, an ingenuousness about his face that spoke of both his ecstasy and violence, or as near to one or the other as he ever got: in short, the sort of guy who freezes for half a second at the sight of a gun in the dark, nowhere innocent enough to suppose the only thing it shoots is water. Had my friend not been a goodlooking redhead I'm not sure this guy would ever have given her the benefit of the doubt. On the other hand, in Boardner's it may be the last ludicrous dream of any failed gangster to die at the hands of a goodlooking redhead.

Another night, not long before boarding my train of liars, I was sitting on the bed watching on television a program about the election. I've followed elections since 1964 when, at the age of fourteen, I was unreservedly and doubtlessly for Barry Goldwater. I haven't been so sure of anything since. In 1968 when I was eighteen I'm sorry to say I would have voted for Richard Nixon, if eighteen-year-olds had then been allowed to vote; as it was, I cast my first presidential vote in 1972 for George McGovern. It remains my most troubled. In 1976 I cast my most hopeful vote for Jimmy Carter, and in 1980 my most futile for John Anderson. My 1984 vote for Walter Mondale was my most disgusted. This year I could conceivably roll all these emotions into one gutwrenching heartbreaking soulchilling act of democracy, though I have no idea which of the candidates would actually elicit such a response. This is the election of the proxy candidates, in which all the candidates running are stand-ins for those who aren't. You vote for Michael Dukakis if you really want Mario

Cuomo, Albert Gore if you really want Sam Nunn, George Bush if you really want Ronald Reagan. Since Richard Gephardt is only a stand-in for Richard Gephardt, it might account for his failure. I began writing about politics in 1984 in a column for a local alternative newspaper, when on the night of the Grammy awards and the New Hampshire primary I set up two small black and white televisions side by side at the foot of the same bed I'm in at this moment, tuning in simultaneously to both events; unfortunately there were some temporal snags. The primary finished at eight o'clock eastern time while the Grammys, held at the same moment five o'clock pacific time, were nonetheless delayed in their broadcast until eight pacific time, which is to say eleven eastern time. I usually adjust to these kinds of warps but this one genuinely undid me. All I know is everything was happening later or earlier than it was supposed to, and that Gary Hart won and so did Michael Jackson, though Walter Mondale and Bruce Springsteen went on to win the nomination while Ronald Reagan and Madonna took the election, an analogy perhaps unfair to Madonna. I covered the Democratic Convention that year for the same paper, the editors of which almost never knew what the hell I was talking about. After reading my Democratic Convention piece my mother, who is still trying to figure out that George McGovern vote, called to ask if I was really so cynical. This was about the time the people who ran the country had come to believe the country was so spiritually empty and intellectually miserable that a "mandate" might be constructed from TV advertisements about the sun rising over a newer, better country for which no one had enough respect to consider defining something resembling even one single moment of a real future. I thought I was the last of the American naïfs.

Cynic then: west of Broadway and south of Boardner's, in the lobby of the Ambassador Hotel, the bellman sells from his small stand slightly shabby goldleafed copies of a book called *Are the Stars Out Tonight?*, the story of the hotel and its adjunct

Coconut Grove. Fifty years ago the Ambassador was the site of Hollywood's most regal occasions, the Academy Awards and the tenancy of Greta Garbo and Rudolph Valentino. Now only the infrequent hotel guests, most of them in their senior years, stroll past the fountains of the lobby to the Palm Bar, where retired private detectives stare out into the east garden. Downstairs, sprawling toward Wilshire Boulevard, is a row of commercial gestures made by the hotel to the modern age—travel agencies and hair salons. In another bar, more ordinary than the Palm, the bartender attends an empty room, talks about his bachelor flat up on Vermont Avenue where he catches the bus to the races on the weekends, and presses on you an old sports magazine with a piece on Joe Louis that he recommends highly. Local legend has it that the Ambassador became a ghost hotel on a very particular night at a very particular moment twenty years ago. At that moment, early in the morning of the fifth of June, Robert Kennedy entered the Ambassador Hotel kitchen, having just left the Ambassador Ballroom, where he had claimed victory in the California presidential primary. In this particular moment the triumph of it all was unimpeachable, an Easterner having wrested the nomination of the Democratic Party in the heathen West. It may be that as Kennedy entered the kitchen he actually looked across it and his mind leapt ahead to that moment when he would exit through the doorway on the other side on his way to his suite. Or it may be that his mind never presumed the luxury of leaping ahead anywhere, given the way things happen later or earlier than they're supposed to, and therefore no interruption could have surprised him. Moreover, it's an occupational hazard not only of running for president but of living in Los Angeles that one does not generally presume the luxury of mentally leaping ahead to doorways of exit, since when the earth moves beneath your feet the doorways move as well. In any case Kennedy was interrupted. He did not reach the Ambassador kitchen's doorway of exit, rather he reached his own doorway of exit. Across the floor of the Other Los Angeles he bled from his torso the Other America. A day later we shipped him back, finished with him as we were, the trail of his blood its own red generic band. In the time since, of course, Los Angeles has given America two presidents, both part of an America which, like so many things in Los Angeles, doesn't exist. This is earthquake country in more ways than one. Now I hear they may tear down the Ambassador; it may have happened by the time you read this. From the collapse may be unleashed a whole new electricity, to live in me with the old, so that the act of breathing, one organ of my body just nudging the other, has the result of a shock.

• • •

It's on the train that I begin the letters. The first one is addressed to Chile's minister of the interior. "To: Señor Sergio Fernandez Fernandez, Ministro del Interior, Palacio de la Moneda, Santiago, Chile. Your Excellency: I am a North American author whose books have been published in the United States and Europe. At the urging of Amnesty International I am writing to respectfully ask that you investigate the abduction of Eliana del Carmen Vargas Diaz, a poverty worker in Santiago who was taken from her neighborhood on 13 December 1987. If she has been detained, I would urge that you establish which agency has taken her, acknowledge her detention and its reasons, and try her quickly before a court or a tribunal. I believe people all over the world, as witnesses to what has happened, wish to be assured by you and your government that Señora Vargas Diaz is being treated humanely. I wish also to express concern about the reported abduction of an unidentified man on 15 December 1987, and ask that the incident be investigated and this man's whereabouts be determined and made public. I thank you for your serious attention to this matter. Steve Erickson." I'm not halfway through this first letter before I realize that I have no faith in it, that I don't believe it's really going to help Señora Vargas Diaz. Still I will write it and send it, and I'll write and send more letters of its kind over the year to come; I'll question whether such a campaign is really addressed to my own pathetic guilt or, worse, my solipsism: even on the radio station in L.A., where I first heard the plea to participate in this action, it was suggested that, if nothing else, such an action will at least make me feel better. I don't know at all that it makes me feel better, and if it does, whether it's sufficient reason to do it. It may even be that such a reason makes the act reprehensible. It may be that this sort of tortured analysis of the act is reprehensible, and that committing it to this page is worse still. But as someone who has distrusted politics in its mass form and the prospect of joining demonstrations even for causes with which I would agree, because the demonstration by its nature must reduce the cause to a moral axiom which can be collectively held, which is to say the cause must be shorn of the very ambiguities that make morality real, then it seems incumbent on me to accept a form of individual demonstration and one particularly suited to a writer. As for including the letters in this book, I'm disinclined to try and make any sort of persuasive case whatsoever as to my own best intentions; let's accept, for the sake of argument, that my intentions are lousy. Let's accept that I'm putting this in the book to grandstand my conscience, or to abuse myself by then demonstrating my cynicism. Let's assume everything about this is twisted, still, it will not help Señora Vargas Diaz *not* to include the letter here, it will not hurt her plight to advertise it, assuming the reader of this book can understand that whatever might be thought of its author's intentions, the world is nonetheless genuinely and truthfully haunted by what it does to those whose consciences warrant more honor than mine. Because Señora Vargas Diaz, like the others for whom I will write letters, is in jail not for any act of violence or revolution but for the quiet expression of a personally held truth, that expression by which humanity bests the beasts in us, day after day after day, in a life of leap days. . . .

• • •

My train was bound to go to New Orleans sooner or later, or I was bound to wind up on a train that did. I arrive at night, in a peculiarly empty station; New Orleans is a town schizophrenic in its fullness and emptiness of life. The cab takes me to the Quarter and I take a room at the St. Peter's Guest House. Considering that a number of the guests have been stashed away by the hotel management in the old servants' quarters of the house, I'm lucky to have a room on the courtyard. I eat dinner at Tujague's and dessert at a place across the street near the Mississippi where they serve the fried holes of donuts. These fried donut holes are quite the thing in New Orleans. Down the street is Storyville, where you can hear blues and jazz. Every bar in the Quarter is teeming with people listening to blues and jazz and sooner or later you're bound to run into someone you know even in this city where you don't know anyone. A few hours before dawn everyone goes home and pulls closed the curtains and sleeps so as to survive the daylight, hoping in the meantime no one invades his sanctum to pound a stake through his heart. By the second night I realize on the banks of the Mississippi that this is one of those places and times where north might be any direction at all; across the river beyond the banks on the other side is a void the extent of which no instinct can determine. When I've been in New Orleans forty-eight hours and will be gone in another thirty-six, I leave Storyville one night having had enough music. The silence of the leaving is uncommon and I relish it, the night having had to fall down its own deep well to get that quiet. I turn off Decatur onto St. Peter Street and walk along the Square. . . .

She could be any age. She could be any color. Sally stands in a hallway behind a pair of shuttered doors not unlike the ones to my own room at my hotel; she calls. Except it isn't me she means. She wears a cape and earrings in the shape of masks on the ends of small scepters, as if they came from France two hundred years ago. *Thomas.* "No," I say, "sorry." I think she's working but when she steps into the street, in as dim a light as the street would offer, I see it isn't like that, it's not in her eyes that she's selling anything. *Thomas?* she says again. "No, I'm not Thomas." She has long straight black hair and under the cape her dress is plain. When she sees I'm not who she wants, she turns quickly to leave and I hear a small metal sound in the road at my feet; that's when I pick up the earring, the mask on the end of the scepter. I think she hears me when I call her, I think she keeps going because she thinks I have the wrong idea, that I've taken her inquiry for something else. She picks up her pace and disappears. Back in my hotel room there is on the small scepter part of the jewel her blood, still slightly wet, as though she pierced her own ear herself.

I see her again two days later, or maybe it's the day after. It's my last day in New Orleans anyway. I'm in a cab leaving a gospel show, I walked out when the minister with his choir blazing behind him finished singing His Blood Is Going To Wash My Sins Away, and then Now I Want To Tell You About My Faith, I Want To Tell You About The Faith Of A Little Girl, You Know What I'm Talking About, I'm Singing About A Town, A Town In Midland Texas, I'm Talking About A Little Girl Named Jessica; and the audience went berserk. I left. In six months a little girl named Jessica in a well in Midland, Texas, has been transformed into Christian myth; I suppose in a way it's reassuring to know the black Christians are as opportunistic as the white ones. I get in a cab and I'm watching from the backseat as we drive through the Garden District where not a single person is to be seen in a window or door or on a porch of any one of the empty mansions that are clean and kept for no one, surrounded by the cut fresh lawns on which no one walks during a single moment that might be witnessed, all the true residents of the city waiting for the rest of us to leave before emerging. Sally is walking on the sidewalk. It's funny that I recognize her imme- diately from the passing cab, having seen her so briefly one or two nights ago in the dark. She wears no cape now. I have in my pocket the earring. I turn in the backseat looking at her, remembering her; and I wouldn't have told the cabdriver to stop if it hadn't been for the blood. I'm thinking about the blood on the scepter and that's when I say, "I need to get out here." He pulls over and I pay him and get out. By now we're a good block and a half beyond where I see her. The sun has fallen and not exactly a fog but a cypress haze is in the air from off the river. I run back to the place. She isn't there and I just sort of walk a ways. Two blocks up in the haze the yellow neon sign of the Chameleon Café is a blotch of dull fire. I turn the corner to pick up the tracks of the St. Charles Trolley which runs from here to Canal Street and back. . . .

On the tracks, rolling toward me from the distance, at a speed a child could outrun, as though it has exhausted its speed somewhere else miles away and now honors only the echo of its old motion, is not a trolley car but a railroad coach. It's disengaged from whatever train or engine it belonged to. I don't know where it came from. Other people on the street look at it a bit peculiarly as well; a black gardener glances up from the last of his watering, his face not registering astonishment exactly, but interest certainly. After a moment the other people on the street, a young couple and a kid on a bike, continue on, and the gardener turns off the water and coils his hose by the door and walks around the house to the back. She and I are the only ones on the street. Sally's half a block up walking along the narrow strip of grass that runs down the street's center, where the St. Charles Line runs as well. She's walking toward the train car, the motion of which just happens to reach the end of its echo at this particular moment that we're here to see it. In one window of the car there's the brief flash of an old man's face before a hand pulls the window closed, I see it too, I'm pretty sure, as Sally does. . . . She puts her hand to her mouth. She leaps onto the steps of the train coach; I'm just standing there in the street with this stupid earring in my hand; I don't think she's even seen me.

I wait a few minutes for her to come off the train, I even walk around the car wondering if she's gotten off another way. After another moment I'm thinking I'll go. I'm thinking about the blood on the earring. Then I step up onto the train. I peer around the corner down the corridor of the car; it's dark and there's no one to be seen, no conductor or attendant or porter, no passenger, no one but her trying to open the door of the compartment where she saw him. The door seems stuck. "Excuse me," I say. She ignores me, gives the door one final jerk, and it opens. *Thomas* she says for the third time I've heard it. I hold back for a while, but I don't have to be too close to see that, beyond the door of the compartment and her just beyond that, no one else is there.

• • •

After New Orleans she appears momentarily in many places, in moments that don't always align themselves with the places so perfectly. The next time I see her is one night south of St. Louis, standing on the wet black grounds outside a concert hall; she's jostled by the people who live by the interstate and have wandered out onto the parking lot to mix with the arriving concert audience. They ask her for money and she asks them for their names. Any one of them might be the one she's looking for. Under the bleachers inside the hall are a hundred homeless people in John Cougar Mellencamp shirts. In the confusion of storms rolling through town, the ragged insurgency infiltrates the event like a virus of the conscience; the homeless have become unspeakably polite. They apologize for bothering you. They're sorry when you reach into your pocket and your extra change gives you a shock; they think the electricity is their fault. I feel them under the bleachers beneath me; at one point when the lights of the hall go down I can stare down through the cracks of the seats and see them waiting out the music, the red dots of their cigarettes glowing silently. Maybe they even like the music.

America's full tonight of a thousand secret audiences waiting beneath the bleachers. The electric shock of change in my pocket seems, in private investigations of the conscience, like a clue. I hear her whispering his name at my feet.

I've seen the man onstage before. Ten years ago at the Whisky on the Sunset Strip in L.A. he called himself Johnny Cougar. He wasn't so impressive as Johnny Cougar. His identity, not to mention his music, was entirely constructed from the identities and music of other artists; this was during the punk era, the most significant contention of which was that you could be what you chose to be as long as the choice was authentic, a contradiction that some found a way to make work. They calculated something from a basic equation that existed somewhere inside them all along, an equation they might never have found or understood had they not permitted themselves or had the culture not permitted them the liberty of calculation. It wouldn't have crossed my mind that Johnny Cougar had a basic equation. It was strange that after Cougar hit his meal ticket with a record called "Jack and Diane," which to anyone else would have justified the fraud of his selfcreation, he changed. He took back his real name. He wrote songs about where he grew up and the people he knew there and what they were losing; most of them were farmers. Secret audiences of the American heart. Even in a business where things happen quickly, Mellencamp's rebirth as himself had an urgency. If his art has none of the ambiguities one hears in similar things by Bruce Springsteen, because as an artist Mellencamp isn't operating on the levels which Springsteen at his most intelligent or inspired might touch all at once, nonetheless Mellencamp can be persuasive in his rage and pride. In his transformation to John Mellencamp, the man who was in the throes of success as Johnny Cougar made his best and bravest decision when he decided to become uncool— which suggests that the basic equation was there all along. But it also proposes that once in a while the most specious promise of

American rock and roll comes true, the promise that it can release you from what you are and reveal some way toward what you want to be. This is why this particular music has never been an art for cynics, who'll dabble in it only when it amuses them cerebrally or offers a trendy payoff.

Unlike Springsteen, who in concert seems clearly destined to what he's become, Mellencamp doesn't seem destined at all, which is why his acclaim and new stature are all the more touching. There are many times in the show when he stares at the ruckus around him in disbelief. For all the maturity of his new work I give him the most credit for doing, early in the show, "Jack and Diane," indicating the perspective and humor about himself that he has achieved growing up. Some people would observe profoundly that rock and roll has achieved it as well, but that's the selfcongratulation of those who've grown not up but old, when people start banishing the memories of youth. Rock and roll's always found perspective about itself at varying and necessary moments in its history; that it's not a cynical art form is what leaves it so open to the wiles and machinations of cynicism. It has a hard time defending itself. Not so long ago, when the wife of one of the men running for president attacked the music before a congressional committee, those who rose to defend it did so by ridiculing its consequence and power: This isn't worth being afraid of, they argued. Thus they hurt the music more than its critics ever did. They supposed they might protect it by trivializing it. Meanwhile across the country a million children offered a defense more eloquent than the music's spokesmen could ever have articulated: they laughed in their parents' faces and turned up the volume.

In fact the congressional committees honored rock and roll with their investigation. They attested to the idea that no matter how assimilated into the mainstream rock seems to have become, Prince's "Darling Nikki" can still be dangerous. "Darling Nikki" is an explicit song about masturbation and, except for what's salacious about it, not one of Prince's more notable efforts. If I were a parent of a teenager listening to "Darling Nikki" I might well be concerned too, perhaps offended. Someday I don't doubt I'll be sitting in front of my television urging on Tipper Gore and maybe comparing her to Eleanor Roosevelt like *The New Republic*. Children never think of sex on their own, of course. They never figure out for themselves what masturbation is. I'm sure I'm the only kid who ever figured this out all by himself. Children would never think of these things at all if it weren't for the influence of songs like "Darling Nikki." Most of the other songs cited before the committee by Mrs. Gore must have had an impact somewhat more subliminal: Springsteen's "I'm On Fire" and Sheena Easton's metaphor-tainted "Sugar Walls," and a large catalog of songs by bands no one's ever heard of, singing lyrics no one ever understood before they were read over national network television to a congressional committee by a woman who wants to be first lady of the United States.

I doubt any congressional committees could much influence John Mellencamp's transformation. Mellencamp doesn't have a lot in common with congressional committees; he's an American. At the core of his Americanism is the release of who he is from what he was; that revelation is beyond the control of the state. It was Jefferson's most significant contention that there are moments when the state must subvert its will to that of the individual spirit; it's bound to offend any number of sensibilities and threaten any number of values. Jefferson deliberately chose to phrase his own basic equation in terms not only of life and liberty but the pursuit of happiness, rather than the life, liberty and property extolled by Locke; he regarded Locke as one of the three greatest men of all time and *still* felt compelled to rewrite him. When Thomas Jefferson invented rock and roll it became the sound of damnation as it existed in the heart of the greatest and guiltiest American who ever lived. It became the sound of release as it existed in the loins of the man who transformed himself in

the thighs of America which went by the name of a fourteen-
year-old slavegirl; and that name was Sally Hemings. . . .

The invention of America sprang from men of furious
sexual torment: Jefferson with his forbidden slave mistress;
Washington who loved a woman who was not his own wife but
the wife of another man; Patrick Henry who kept his insane wife
locked in his basement at the very moment he pleaded for death
if not liberty; Thomas Paine whose first wife died in childbirth so
that he believed he'd killed her, and thus was impotent with his
second wife who chose to advertise this failure throughout the
community, and in the shame of which Paine wrote his fiercest
pamphlets. The invention of America by these men was meant to
spring them loose from the bonds of afterlife; it redefined us not
as instruments of God or heaven but rather as the incarnations of
our memories of our own selves. Tonight I'm the memory of
someone on a train to Chicago. I ride through the memories of
this person on this train, across plains that stretch through the
Midwest; I record in vivid and relentless detail every important
memory of the years to come. When my existence ceases as the
incarnation of the memories of others, I will cease; in a country
where men are the incarnations of memory, fame becomes a
work of art unto itself. This isn't to suggest it hasn't been true in
other times and places. The fame of Jesus was the creation of
both Jesus and his audience, an act in which the audience
became aggressively engaged, injecting into the subsequent
memory and its word of mouth something of themselves. But
America is the apotheosis of this, where memory itself is a
country, because America is where only memory divides the
present from the future, and where the unconscious dreams of
the people who live here understand that the Declaration of
Independence was signed after Hiroshima, not before, and
neither has yet happened. Nowhere but in rock and roll, the
music of Jefferson's damnation and desire, is the art-creation of
fame, the artifact of personal transformation, so manifest. What

in Elvis Presley so embodies the meaning of rock and roll if not his creation of his own fame, his greatest act as an artist? For most of his career Elvis Presley didn't even *like* rock and roll. With the exception of several electrifying moments in the late 1960s, he spent the last seventeen years of that career singing himself away from the first six. In the history of rock and roll Chuck Berry, John Lennon, Bob Dylan, Otis Redding, Ray Charles, Aretha Franklin have all possessed gifts and visions as great; but none, except in his own way Lennon, created a work of art comparable to the one Presley created in his own fame, and if Lennon is the exception it's partly by an American act of violence, hot metal splashing Lennonmemory on the walls of New York. . . .

The democratization of fame in America is like redistribution of wealth: it attempts to eliminate the possibility of being obscure as the other would eliminate the possibility of being poor. Where fame was once reputation based on public estimation, which in turn was once based on some achievement or merit, now people become famous for nothing but talking to famous people on television; in the end it's not really true that in the future everyone will be famous for fifteen minutes. Rather, everyone will be *familiar* for fifteen minutes, sharing a common recognizability that means something only to the recognized and nothing to those who do the recognizing. We've democratized our perception of someone like Ronald Reagan to the point that, even if we regard him favorably, it's impossible to magnify him to the dimension of someone who conjured in the consciousness something grander. Franklin Roosevelt's fame belonged to us. Elvis Presley's may have been the last that belonged to us, though I'm not certain but that some effort of his to seize it back from us and own it wholly himself killed him. Ronald Reagan's fame belongs utterly to himself, he's entirely comfortable with our passivity to it. He not only survives our passivity but flourishes in it. We react to his fame but, unlike his media advisers and image makers, we have no personal investment in it, no role in creating a more resonant fame beyond sheer recognizability and recognizability's attendant power. By the time you read this you won't even remember who I'm talking about; no public person will ever have vanished so quickly from the mind. Who's he talking about? you're asking yourself at this very moment. Once we remembered him as the president of the United States; we began forgetting in Leap Year, the year all insignificant memories vanish in a twenty-four-hour phantom.

It's as impossible for Ronald Reagan to rise above our mundane perception of him as it is for Jesus to dip below the communal mythos of his reputation, which has reached such a pitch over the centuries that we've saturated Jesus with ourselves whether we accept his divinity or not. There's nothing of the actual Jesus left. As a work of fame-art, the only American who's come close to matching Jesus' impact and calculation was Lincoln, with a comparable eye for opportunity and a history of personal failure so searing and self-destructive that what constituted a crisis for the nation—civil war—was for him something of a lucky break. The schemes by which Lincoln resurrected himself from a shattered career and endeared his image to the public at large, like growing hair on his face, were not so distant from the manipulative spirit of a candidate changing his name or the way he signs it; but Lincoln created his fame with the help of history and the coercion of events. It also helped that he could keep his values straight amid the conniving, though this might have been easier to do when values could be formulated in private, considered and abridged and supplemented for days or even weeks out of the eye of the public before technology put a man on daily display. Public scrutiny didn't then make the evolution of a personal value system appear so nakedly opportunistic. We now so equate the fraudulence and authenticity of what we see on television that we're entirely willing to elect a set of values as dramatically rendered as Reagan's even when we understand that it's only part of the choreography of personality.

This isn't to say that Reagan hasn't meant the things he's said. It's to say that those things can't be held as the expression of something fundamental in him, a basic equation, because there's never been any evidence of a basic equation to be expressed. We elected a man to play Ronald Reagan. That he's persisted in doing it so well has remained the foremost measure by which we've judged him.

This is what makes so acceptable the difference between what Reagan says and does. The occasional shouts against the mirage that have found utterance over the years haven't fallen on deaf ears: we've heard them. Walter Mondale was defeated four years ago not because he wouldn't have been a particularly good president but because of the way he failed, as Reagan has succeeded, in greasing the wheels of America's self-image. Of what memory that we could possibly want to remember would Walter Mondale have served as incarnation? His election would have left the country a psychological shambles; it would have left unclear whether we're really a good people or care about being one. Reagan is the Rorschach that answered the question. We haven't cared much recently about being a good people; we're not into it. We prefer the memory of a rich people or a safe people. In America's basic equation there's been room for a hundred contradictions between what Ronald Reagan said about the budget and how he busted it, what he said about drug dealers and how he colluded with them, what he said about the environment and how he savaged it, what he said about individual opportunity and how his policies subverted it, what he said about individual freedom and how his attorney general laid siege to it, the role he played as leader and the way he chose to lead, which was never to ask the people to do anything that wasn't easiest for the majority of them, or to accept any truth they didn't want to accept. Reagan the American bludgeoned our love of the truth into the pulp of his own biases and our love of justice into the muck of his own phobias. The day he became Our American, I became a nomad, on a train across a field of memory. Let's not pretend we elected him in spite of his contradictions and hypocrisies: we chose him for them.

It's a facile conceit among those on the Left that Reagan's just an actor who became president. The truth is he's a political genius who happened once to be an actor, and to try and trivialize him in other terms is the sort of tactic with which his enemies have rendered themselves impotent against him. It's also unfair to Reagan, and a delusion not only of his enemies but his supporters as well, to trivialize the part his movie career played in the presidency we chose him for. I'm fully prepared to accept the prospect that the memories Ronald Reagan holds, of history that was invented on the soundstages of Los Angeles forty years ago, are genuine memories for him, with as much resonance as reality and perhaps a good deal more. We elected those memories because they're ours too; they mark our clocks more than any mere numbers. Because Ronald Reagan was always rehearsing to be Ronald Reagan, in a way not unlike John Cougar rehearsing to be John Mellencamp, his performance is touched by conviction, the difference being that John Cougar was always John Mellencamp in the first place, somewhere down inside him. Reagan rehearsed himself into the role written by others and in at least two instances of his presidency the actor and the role became one, as they say. The first was when someone shot him. In such a moment Ronald Reagan played the Ronald Reagan he'd rehearsed for all his life, and the result was a small movie unto itself, in which he played at courage and grace and humor with all the courage and grace and humor of a good actor playing himself. I do not intend to dismiss the incident when I say this. This was a man shot and in peril, inventing himself with genius in order to survive and, in the process, creating a piece of fame. The political consequences of it are impossible to overestimate: a presidency was salvaged by the extra months that came flowing to it through a hole in time put there by a man who would make

Jodie Foster his slave. In the depths of 1982, when there was a recession and Reagan wasn't so popular, who's to say what those extra months may have won, what they were worth? The second instance where Reagan's lifelong rehearsal to be Reagan paid off was the day the space shuttle Challenger found oblivion in the skies of Florida. Reagan's subsequent address to the nation was the most eloquent of his presidency, and the moment when Americanmemory, ripped with a burning gash as perilous as the one John Hinckley's gun made in the president, needed whatever psychic balm would mend it: could anyone have addressed himself to it with the genius of Reagan? This was such a moment for which no presidency other than Ronald Reagan's was made, and it wasn't simply the speech itself: Jimmy Carter could have made the same speech, but Carter's presence would have rendered the Challenger explosion not American tragedy but American failure, in the same way Carter's presence rendered so many things failures, rightly or wrongly, in the same way Carter could never have gotten away with so many things Ronald Reagan did—dead Marines back from Lebanon and arms deals with the Islam that humiliates us.

Once, fifteen years ago, my girlfriend learned her mother was dying of cancer. . . . The time between the moment we learned what was festering in her brain and the moment she died was four months; the nightmare of life was concentrated and focused. The girl had a younger brother with cerebral palsy and there was no father, so responsibility for the boy fell to her and her sisters. For four months I was in the middle of life at its least artificial, and confronted at the age of twenty-three with an array of guilt and dilemma, fantasies of flight and abandonment, revelations of obligation and the ensuing realization that my guilt could only be a fraction of what was really at stake: I might walk away any moment, bound to the situation by nothing but conscience. Fifteen months after the girl's mother died I did walk away, for reasons that had since removed themselves from the bonds of conscience. During the four months I wrote about it in my head. Not on paper but in my head. Every tragic piece of news became a part of the story I told myself; I rendered it all fiction. It was fiction for which I was rehearsing, creating the characters of those who die and live with dying. At the time I thought it was appalling. There are times I still find it appalling. I question what devices of distance are at work in such a situation, when a writer writes the terrible things he lives, and the way he writes it becomes more real to him than the way he lives it. In the most terrible tragedies of love affairs and dilemmas that have presented themselves since, even in moments when the better part of me feels the anguish due them, the writer writes, not so different from the actor who acts or the politician who transforms the stuff of his ego into fame-art. The final paradox will come when someday an actor plays Ronald Reagan in a movie, which is to say he will play Ronald Reagan playing Ronald Reagan. How will he do this? One may ask this of the actor who plays Jesus or Hitler, the mere actor who, presumably absorbed in the creation of his own fame, rebuilds before our eyes the instruments of persona and mesmerization that made up the fame of someone like Jesus; when an actor goes that far in a performance it seems only another step to becoming Jesus himself. People like Jesus or Lincoln or Hitler were men whose identities motivated their drive rather than the other way around; they clung willfully to the precipice of their destinies even as history stood overhead and stomped on their fingers. How unnerving it is for the actor, in the exploration of a role, to understand what it was like to be Jesus, who himself believed he understood what it was like to be God? And as scary as it must be to discover one's empathetic bond with a god, what is it like for the actor who plays Hitler, navigating the human spirit's most fuliginous corridors to arrive at his own monstrosity? Only the most ruthless artist would do such a thing, at which point he might be not steps from becoming Hitler, but millimeters. But in

Ronald Reagan's case, his drive motivated his identity, such as it was, and we must therefore question whether Ronald Reagan ever really understood what it was like to be the person he was playing, Ronald Reagan.

In the end, the most profound thing about a historic performance isn't how it confounds the audience but rather how it galvanizes it, demanding that it forfeit its passivity: Ronald Reagan never demanded this forfeiture, which is why his performance won't live in our hearts and minds beyond the moment he leaves us. Sooner or later, faced with the famous reality and all the surfaces that reflect it, the audience will determine the difference only by coming out from beneath the bleachers and becoming an active part once more in the creation of fame; the price of such a proposition may include your fifteen minutes and mine. This assumes the audience still cares enough to reach out and feel for itself which image is solid and which one's hand passes through unobstructed. We build our actors churches these days, and elect our surfaces to the highest office in the land. We're left to make distinctions between fame and familiarity, between the fame-art that's the product of an original vision and the fame-art of the fake, who can re-create a Jesus or a president the way some fakes re-create Picassos or Chagalls or rich men's memoirs.

• • •

Not far from Chicago my train comes to Marceline, Missouri, hometown of Walt Disney. We've been reminded of this momentous stop ever since the journey began, and I've been advised that once I've seen Marceline it will be clear where the Disney vision came from. . . . My brother-in-law comments that my nephew at the age of four has already come to discriminate between Disney and other cartoons; the others, in my nephew's eyes, aren't cartoons at all, in the way runes aren't art but mere language. My nephew marvels at the way buds will flower on a

Disney tree as a bird flies by, a leap of faith in cause-and-effect physics that Disney understood and communicated and integrated into his worldview. Disney is one of the century's great conceptual artists if art is defined by the exchange of realities between artist and audience. That the pristine control Disney exerted over that art is obsessive at the least and twisted at most, or that the moral vision of that art harbors its own creepy malevolence, doesn't diminish the genius involved. From the window of my compartment Marceline looks a little banal; I don't think Disney found his darkness here, or his abyss, and like all artists of the nuclear imagination, Disney wasn't anything without his abyss; his cause-and-effect faith didn't mean much. . . .

It's curious but in fact logical that in the nuclear age a nuclear imagination is shared by so few; our imaginations remain conventional, stunted by the temptation to render the abyss unimaginable. By nuclear imagination I mean that poetry that Einstein conceived and compelled us to accept in the face of empiricism, in the way that Einstein's enigmas of time and space are accepted without anyone's having the slightest certainty they're actually true. He arrived at them less through a process of empiricism than muse, since mere empiricism never led anyone to such conclusions; by reason, Einstein's conclusions should be dismissable. Their form is manifested empirically by not much more than the sights of Marceline, a schoolhouse and park, a grove of apple trees. But as with all great poetry, reason can make neither the originality of such conclusions nor the images they evoke go away, and instead they fix themselves first in the collective consciousness, then the collective memory, then the genetic memory of the species. Because the tenets of that reason are heavier than the empiricism of science can bear, they result in the kind of inevitabilities only art can verify. Einstein had a nuclear imagination before there was ever nuclear fission; he caught the whiff of something in the air nearly forty years before the first ash. He may or may not have given thought at that moment to nuclear holocaust but he already had an intuition for its ramifications. He was already touched by the way its pending presence altered the times. People with nuclear imagination not only conceive of the abyss and confront it, but are liberated by it; everything they do is infused with the blood of an armageddon with no god, a judgment day in which the guilty and the innocent are damned with equal cosmic merriment. They dance along the edge of the abyss to banish their dread of falling over, relishing the view that their position on the edge affords, daring the ground to shift beneath their feet. They can't be bothered with pretending the edge isn't there. They won't be paralyzed by it. They'll take a running start toward it only to stop inches away while the crowd gasps in horror. In the process they force the crowd to consider matters as they do, confronted with the truth that every moment is potentially irrevocable.

The nuclear imagination isn't simply the heightened aware-ness of the doom, it's the relationship one establishes with doom. Billie Holiday had nuclear imagination but Judy Garland didn't: doom raped Judy while Billie managed to get on top, humping doom to the last orgasmic throe. When she died she took doom with her, or at least its vital parts. Among nuclear American authors two endemic concepts, the end of Man and the end of the Word, have produced not a great literature but an ironic one: in the face of these looming eventualities, the first made real by the Bomb and the second by television, American literature decided it was left with no psychological recourse but a sense of relieved contempt, an inner reassurance that nothing we write can be of import, that nothing we invent can measure up to global inventions of self-destruction. In August 1945 the human imagination consumed itself, the literary imagination calcifying accordingly and not with resistance but in a rush. The Bomb was the perfect out for writers intimidated by their own obsolescence. As the American novel of the Twenties and Thirties was the dominant literary expression of its time, the American novel of the nuclear era has institutionalized an estranged and futile hip consciousness that becomes ours by inheritance. By "ours" I mean not simply the weathered and future-racked ex-beats and hippies among us but the generation of writers that has followed, growing up with a television culture the most pernicious influence of which is not its inanity or even its visuality but that visuality's want of metaphor, the niggling literalness of its archetypes. We've insisted on writing as though we expect never really to mean anything to anyone again, as though with an unstated loathing for anyone who would value what we say. Afraid of seeming sentimental, we've risked no passion; afraid of seeming pretentious, we've risked no scope. We've written little books that masquerade as large ones, literature for the blackboards, appalled by its own juices, that doesn't deserve to capture the imagination of the public because it has none of its own to offer in return. Thus the great American authors of the nuclear imagination are those who wedded themselves to something more primitive than technology could touch, that invaded a land beyond technology, which is to say the great American novels of the last thirty-five years have had titles like Chuck Berry's *Great Twenty-Eight* and *Blonde on Blonde* by Bob Dylan, *Where Are You* by Frank Sinatra and *What's Going On* by Marvin Gaye, Bruce Springsteen's *The River* and *Little Richard's Grooviest 17 Original Hits!*

Which isn't to suggest that the nuclear imagination is in itself a moral property. Gandhi had it, but so did Hitler, who never even lived to see the first nuclear bomb. Stalin, on the other hand, two or three times the monster Hitler was if one measures barbarism in mere corpses, did not have nuclear imagination; his style of evil was prosaic compared with the baroque flourishes of Hitler's human lampshades. In the realm of politics not many major figures have nuclear imagination, because to a large extent their political fates depend on the perpetuation of what the conventional imagination is comfortable with; and those with nuclear imagination remain fated to the oblivion which is integral to the vision they're trying to define. The exceptions are usually so notably flamboyant we can regard them only as saintly aberrations, if we perceive them as good, or as demonic, if we perceive them as evil. Of our modern presidents, Richard Nixon had the most nuclear imagination by far. Except perhaps for John Kennedy, he was probably the only one to have any at all. With Nixon, absolutely nothing was out of the question. No petty mean thing was too dreadful, no grand breathtaking gesture too wonderful. He was always establishing his position in relation to the abyss, he never really cared whether the world went up in smoke, only how it might char his own legacy. Thus as president he was free of constraints, including those of his own warlike instincts, and thus he was free to end bad wars however slowly, reconcile with China, impose the most stringent economic controls since the Great Depression, conjure an international atmosphere of trilateral stability, conjure a domestic atmosphere of police repression, subvert the country's mechanisms of justice and his own seat of power, and cry about his mom on TV. A first-rate example of someone with an extremely dramatic conventional imagination but no nuclear imagination at all is Ronald Reagan. With all the talk in the early days of his administration about nuclear superiority and limited nuclear exchanges and winnable nuclear wars, the chasm between the conventional imagination and the nuclear became evident in a way it never had before. Reagan imported into the Eighties fresh wet slabs of fear the likes of which no one had seen in twenty or thirty years.

It's not to minimize the achievement of Reagan's later treaties with Mikhail Gorbachev or the jaunty eccentricity of his plan to build an all-protective space shield, to point out these are the expressions of a grand conventional imagination rather than one which fundamentally shuffles the reference points of space and time. By our definition of the concept, it's impossible to say Reagan was ever liberated by the abyss when he wouldn't even see it, let alone acknowledge it somewhere in his soul; he always thought the abyss was a gully off to the side of the road. He thought he was going to put on his army fatigues and helmet and walk across. In the early days of his administration when Reagan was always touring battleships and watching jets through binoculars, you knew he just wanted to be president so he could salute everything. His genius lay in his ability to open up the scenarios of the conventional imagination in a way that accommodated what became unavoidable: and with the treaties and the Strategic Defense Initiative as well, he embraced the conviction as it's always been held by political convention that the abyss is bombs. The abyss is not bombs. The abyss is the doomsday impulse that produced the bombs. The abyss is the nuclear imagination itself, which stares into its own image. Should every bomb in the world disappear in this moment, the rush would then be on to build the first bomb again, and use it on whoever is frantically building the second bomb. The elimination of bombs will lop off the hands of a beast blistered by the doomsday impulse, at which point he bares his fangs instead. The edge of the abyss is here forevermore. The conventional imagination is left to choose between pretending it can unlearn what it knows or accepting the abyss as the shoreline that will never change. There's no moving back inland. On this beach we stay alive by the mutuality of our nightmares.

While John Kennedy and Richard Nixon were both in some way touched by nuclear imagination, and Robert Kennedy was rapidly evolving one, it wasn't until 1984 that a major fullblown candidate of the nuclear imagination bid for the presidency. His name was Gary Hart. In the political history of the United States that was once America, Hart's explosion will be viewed as a fast and finite one, a nova in which jagged light erupted and flooded one horizon to the other with a white glow that rushed back to black. In such moments you learn to look around you quickly and see what can be seen while you have the chance. Hart's candidacy of New Ideas was a misnomer for what was in fact a sensibility defined by the abyss, and liberated by it: a sensibility of consequence in a country that has learned to dread consequence, having convinced itself over forty years that the ultimate consequence was either totalitarian rule or atomic obliteration. These were the years that the country, having lost its faith in consequence, lost its faith in the impulse from which the country was born: that there could be people who bonded themselves to the idea that every day was dangerous and meant to be so. That every day the consequences of passion and courage and justice were there to be fulfilled or betrayed, and no recourse existed between the two. Nothing about America was meant to be comfortable or timid. Consequence was everything: every word and idea was a bomb. The abyss was that single extra mutant day in which lived the whole history of the idea of America from the beginning: 1776 was Leap Year too. But when in the nuclear age the ultimate consequence became too awful to consider—and no small consequence exists that isn't linked to the next, and no chain of consequences exists without the ultimate one lurking at its dark end—the spirit of the American idea withered and died, sometimes by the malice of those who hated America, sometimes by the mean greed of those who most claimed to love it, usually by the indifference of those who loved it as a matter of rote or habit, which is to say most of us.

Somehow people understood immediately, intuitively, that Hart was a candidate of consequence, born just prior to the first light of the nuclear age and uprooted by it, yanked from his time by the scruff of his soul. When it was impossible for the public to quite name this suggestion of consequence—probably even Hart himself couldn't name it—it described the phenomenon another way, which was to say that Hart was crazy. Usually it wasn't stated this baldly; psychological euphemisms were employed, visual metaphors of flashing red telephones in the television advertisements of Hart's opponent, Walter Mondale. But crazy was what it meant, and there was nothing necessarily slanderous about it, because it was true. Gary Hart is mad, possessed of a political vision that bubbled up from that piece of America, or the abyss, he carries inside him; and for five weeks in the winter of 1984, as Hart won one primary or caucus after another away from Mondale, the country tapped into its deep lurking nuclear imagination. Mondale's subsequent success was to haunt conventional concerns and argue, If you play that close to the edge, you may fall off. Better come back. People came back. Sensing that Hart was one of those people with whom almost anything was possible, and accepting him for it, they then quibbled. For five years commentators in the press cited one thing about Gary Hart above all else as indicative of his fundamental corruption, and that was the dropping of a syllable from his name; the artificiality of people's sense of identity is such that they assume the name their parents give them is more legitimate than one they choose for themselves. The schizophrenia of America is that nowhere else do people choose new identities for themselves more readily, and nowhere else does the public more adore and despise them for it. In past centuries people's names were the spoken telegrams of where they'd come from and therefore who they'd been; this was a time when people were extensions of the very earth beneath them. In America, roots are the things which bind people and hold them down. People rip the roots out, and then romanticize what's been severed, in the same way Americans always romanticize that of themselves they've destroyed: English royalty, the Confederacy, Billy the Kid.

Hart tore himself free of his roots but refused to romanticize them, though he might not have been above using them politically. In that refusal he was a candidate of consequence unlike any other, because the implication of the way he had destroyed something of himself was that there is always a price to be paid for everything: a truth that the ancient Americans understood best of all and which the citizens of the United States understand least. Ronald Reagan became the most popular politician of a generation by never exacting a price from anyone except those too weak to protest, and was acclaimed a model of leadership by never asking the people to do a single thing they didn't want to. Because of what the Ultimate Consequence has become in the nuclear age, the potential that Hart's madness offered evoked with it the price that madness might entail; you can't blame people for being afraid of it. The people would be afraid of Jefferson or Lincoln as well, the latter racked by nightmares and premonitions and breakdown, the former verging on the completely pixilated at his most benign, and anarchic at his darkest. This kind of madness defies literal thinking, and when it defied a literal explanation for Gary Hart, an alternate explanation was contrived and presented in its place, which was that Hart was a phony, something the press had created even as the press was questioning what Hart had created for himself. None of us is charmed to consider the particular truth, which is that we the people have become the phonies. We were phonies when we elected Jimmy Carter and we were phonies when we elected Ronald Reagan, both of whom turned out to be exactly the kind of men we claimed to want when we chose them. We decided we hated Carter when in essence we hated ourselves for ever wanting the political innocence he offered; we'll never forgive him for it, and we'll eventually come to despise Reagan for the same reason. By the same token, when Hart came the closest he'll ever come to the presidency during those five weeks in 1984, we saluted his selfinvention because it offered the opportunity to reinvent ourselves; but in the end we weren't ready for the opportunity. It meant giving up that of ourselves which we know, even if it's that of ourselves which we despise.

As opposed to someone like Hart, the phonier the candidate of the conventional imagination becomes, the more successful: Reagan is the best example, but Walter Mondale was also a good

one in the spring primaries of 1984, and Missouri congressman
Richard Gephardt is an even better one in the campaign of 1988.
We can somehow live with these men being fakes, and sometimes
it's only in the momentary vision of a nova like Hart's that we see
a whole new Reagan or Mondale or Gephardt altogether. With
each passing moment they look less and less like we thought they
did; when the nova goes out completely, they glow in the dark as
someone else entirely. In 1984 Hart came very close to blowing
Mondale out of the sky. In that year's smaller, earlier version of
what would be called Super Tuesday, Mondale took a mere two
states, the second, Georgia, by a couple of thousand votes. Had
he lost Georgia he could not have sustained a major candidacy
going into the Illinois primary which followed. Mondale's
candidacy was saved by the very man who had given it justification in the first place, Mondale's old employer Jimmy Carter,
who endorsed and campaigned for Mondale in his home state
where such an effort still had value. It seems ungenerous, when
recent political history has already been so ungenerous to him, to
suggest Carter might therefore bear some responsibility for still a
second and worse Democratic debacle; but there it is: Gary Hart
wouldn't have beaten Reagan in 1984 either, but he would have
carried more than a single state—say, ten to twelve—and lost by
a margin closer to eight than eighteen. In March of that year a
Gallup poll showed Hart running ahead of Reagan by nine
percent—dubious, to be sure, but indicative of the shadows of
doubts that people already harbored about Reagan, and how in
the glare of the nova they will, if only for a moment, actually
consider banishing the source of those shadows. . . .

By 1987, preparing for another run at the presidency and
better positioned to capture the office than anyone else in the
country, Hart offered a programmatic blueprinted future, as
though to ground his madness in responsibility. But the revelations of Hart's nova remained the same as three years before: a
government at the abyss, in a state of consequence, in which the

state itself is an entity of no innate moral property, neither to be warded off as evil by the political Right nor embraced as good by the political Left, except as the morality of circumstances and the original American idea dictate. In retrospect it seems probable that Hart himself had a failure of nerve, though the famous theories of self-destruction would have more ,credibility if the episode which undid him was something other than the one with Donna Rice. We'll never know. After the episode we were entertained by wellpaid writers in tony New York magazines whose long psychological contemplations and excavations of the id were dedicated to explaining why a man would want to have sex with a good-looking blonde with large breasts. Some would not need an extremely sophisticated theory to account for such a thing. The Judgment Question became a stalking horse for those who felt uncomfortable moralizing about Hart's marital fidelity, to the effect that it was the man's own business what sort of sex life he chose to lead but that he didn't have to be so stupid about it, and this would reflect how smartly or stupidly he might act as president. I offer now an answer: he wanted her. He wanted the good-looking blonde and, like most men who have the blood and semen of the present coursing through them rather than the embalmment of historical retrospection, he wanted her at that moment more than he wanted the most power this earthly existence can give to a man. You might think this would be to his credit. You might think this would be reassuring that the hunger for something human was not utterly subject to the hunger for political power, that something mattered to him more than the smooth glassy feel of the Ultimate Consequence at his fingertips. I personally distrust anyone who thinks straight in such circum-stances: how is it we've become so calculated as to regard the most irrational of acts, sex, as an exalted standard of rational behavior? In the 1790s George Washington's secretary of the treasury, Alexander Hamilton, was compromised by a prostitute in a blackmail scheme. Hamilton was as ambitious and brilliant an American as ever lived. He was the second most powerful man in the country and aspired night and day to be the first; his greatest dream was to succeed to the throne of an American monarchy. Almost nothing else mattered even remotely as much; and yet in moments, at the peril of his career and reputation and ambition, a woman he himself called a slut mattered more. Even after the blackmail scheme unfolded he continued to see the woman, for many more months: his life then was studded with moments in which having her meant more than all the other things his life had come to mean, as the life of his greatest foe, Jefferson, had its many moments over the years when having Sally Hemings meant as much to him. Before the splendors of Marilyn Monroe, John Kennedy apparently felt the same. Rumor has it that this is the way the world turns. It's not to say it's admirable behavior, or behavior that doesn't deserve reproach, but it also has nothing to do with the caprices of admirable leadership. Certainly Gary Hart's affair with Donna Rice didn't demonstrate good judgment, but Ronald Reagan has demonstrated worse judgment more times than might be noted here, not to mention other instances of bad judgment evident throughout recent American politics. Al Gore marrying Tipper, for instance. Now that was bad judgment.

Apparently those people who condemned the affair with Rice not on moral grounds but for its bad judgment would have felt much better about Gary Hart if, confronted with his sexual desire, he had said, I'm going to walk away from this, not because it's adultery and therefore I shouldn't do it, but because it doesn't fit in with my political ambitions. For myself, I would have felt much worse about such a person. For myself, I can hardly think of anything more inhuman, I can hardly think of anyone I'd less like to see with the fate of the world in his hands. My suspicion is that Hart pursued the affair not despite the way it jeopardized his political plans but because of it. I know this sounds as trite and glib as all the other psychoanalyses, and I didn't buy it until the 1988 race began to unfold after Hart reentered it last December. A pattern became clear: Hart seemed to flourish when his situation was hopeless, dating back to 1984 when Hart did best when his chances were slimmest. This was in the early days of the 1984 Iowa caucuses and the New Hampshire primary that followed; after that, as he was well on his way to the nomination, his performance became more and more disappointing until, in one debate preceding the Southern contests, Mondale asked him where the beef was. This has been widely considered the blow that brought down Hart, a scathingly ingenious witticism based on a current hamburger commercial. In fact, it was not the first time the line had been used about Hart: Lane Kirkland, the head of the AFL-CIO, had said the very same thing to a rally the night before. Since Mondale was already viewed as kowtowing to organized labor, Hart's natural riposte was obvious: "What, are the unions even writing your jokes for you now, Fritz?" Except that Hart didn't make that riposte, I made it, sitting in front of my television set watching Hart nod in earnest while the audience laughed at him. Not until later in the spring, when Hart's chances of taking the nomination were utterly gone, did he rebound, winning most of the final primaries including California's.

In December 1987, having seven months before shut down his 1988 campaign, Hart relaunched it when its prospects seemed foolish; the man seemed more alive on the occasion of this second announcement than he had on the occasion of the first the previous April. In January, in a televised conference at the Kennedy School of Government at Harvard, before a gathering of students and professors, Hart spoke to both the rationale and concerns of his new candidacy, and in the process presented a large picture of the world and the times, the intricacy and completeness of which humbled virtually everyone else in the presidential race. It was a show of intellectual command that was somehow enhanced rather than diminished by the fact that during the entire program there could be seen, directly over Hart's right shoulder, a beautiful blonde whose gaze smoldered somewhere between fascination and fury. The very image filled out the picture of Gary Hart and also put it in perspective: it was as though Hart was saying, Yeah, I know she's there, but right now *this* is what we're talking about. And should the perspective have eluded anyone, there was still the inevitable question from the audience about judgment, to which Hart responded with an angry litany about the administration of the past seven years, in which Ronald Reagan had shown appalling judgment about one matter or another. Watching it then, and watching the tape of it now, months later, it has struck me that it would have been an entirely worthwhile investment, should it have been at all possible in the quagmire of Hart's money problems, to send a couple of thousand tapes around the country to whoever might still be open enough to be impressed by it.

Yet after Hart caught everyone's imagination by reentering the race—I heard people who'd never liked Hart express admiration for the sheer gall of it—he began to run not on his own terms but the terms of others, and everything fell away from him. Obviously it isn't to say those terms lacked justification; rather it's to say that Hart was miserably ineffective running on those terms, and this was never more evident than in the Des Moines debate of mid-January, the first among the Democratic debates to include Hart. For this debate Hart made the clear decision to speak to people's worries about his character: remembering the heat of his answer in the Harvard interview, and how it knocked the audience for a loop, he tried to parlay this response into a debating point, where it had no power at all. It sounded contrived and false, and except for Hart's performance in the 1984 New York primary, where he pandered shamelessly to the Jewish vote, his distinction between private morality and public morality was the most bogus moment of his political career. It was very much of a piece with comparisons Hart made between himself and various unfaithful American presidents; the point was accurate but coming from Hart all these things sounded like excuses, and rendered his flaws more graceless. After that first debate one knew immediately and instinctively that it was over for Gary Hart. Not only did what he said reinforce the contention of many that he was synthetic, but his performance didn't diminish the other candidates on the forum with him, as many expected it would. A couple, particularly Michael Dukakis and Richard Gephardt, compared rather well. The press, which has always deeply despised Hart—the literality of the press necessarily makes it a function of their job to despise someone like Hart—relished his failure and went on to report the following week a new irregularity in his campaign funding, though it was a minor story in which Hart was not personally culpable as far as anyone could tell. Later, when Hart had utterly collapsed in the Iowa and New Hampshire returns, one news commentator who four years earlier had tried to coax Hart into doing a Ted Kennedy imitation on network television reported that his faith in the people had been restored, given their verdict on Hart: his hatred of Hart was palpable.

In political ruins, scorned as a pariah, Hart proceeded unnoticed to fare much better in the debates that followed. Almost invisibly, he won the first major debate in Houston that followed the New Hampshire primary; he stopped speaking to the character questions and spoke rather to his own ideas. He also laughed a lot. He rolled his eyes at a particularly insufferable moment from Gore, though from Gore there were always many such moments to choose from, and he imitated Gephardt in a fingerpointing exchange chortling the whole time he did it while Gephardt just took it all more and more seriously. ("Your thinking is stuck in the past, Gary." "No, Dick, *your* thinking is stuck in the past." "No, Gary, *your* thinking." "No, Dick. . . .") Hart was also left a role to play after the exit of Bruce Babbitt, a former governor of Arizona whose candidacy became untenable when people began to recognize the ominous traits of a smart and responsible president; that recognition wasn't in contradiction to Babbitt's poor showing in the early contests but rather was symbiotic with it. Both recognition and failure were based on the same thing. Babbitt simply couldn't distort either himself or the truth in the ways that the modern presidency of the United States, rather than America, calls for; and he must remain satisfied with his place in history as one of the better presidents we never had. In the Houston debate there were at least four or five instances where the surviving candidates, which was everyone except Babbitt, kept referring to him; never has a loser been so extolled in one place at one time in terms of so much respect by so many winners who had beaten him. Now Hart took up several of Babbitt's themes. Babbitt, who was chagrined by Hart's contention on reentering the race that no one else was saying anything, must have been even more chagrined to have become Hart's mentor—though Babbitt's sense of irony is such that he might also have been amused. At any rate Hart became the gadfly, understanding he was at rock bottom, ground zero, not simply over the edge of the abyss but slithering around down in the rubble, and therefore saying things and challenging the fated ones in a fashion that had them wincing, contorting and shifting in their seats. Whether it was the incisive intelligence of what he said, or just the smell of a political corpse, the corpse of one who a year before seemed destined to become president, the others hung in and waited for the arctic winds of oblivion to come and blow the remains of him and his fucking questions out of sight and out of mind.

"I think," someone said to me in a bar around that time, "the American people are on some level profoundly disappointed that Gary Hart is not going to be president." I don't know whether this is true. Since the person who said this was not an American but a younger European who'd been living here for some years, it for some reason had a greater impact than it might have otherwise. If it's so, then surely with the disappointment there's profound relief as well, not so much for what of Gary Hart we were spared but for what of ourselves we were spared, the wild shot in the nuclear dark, a country that names itself, full of people that name themselves always believing that in the act of self-naming the name is only a lie. Twelve weeks after entering the race again, after half the states in the nation had in the course of their caucuses and primaries given Hart not a single delegate, Hart took himself out again with a humor that might have served him better had it been more in evidence before; perhaps he felt relief as well. Someone asked him if he would ever run for president again. "Not this year," he answered deadpan, then laughed maniacally. "I think twice in one year's enough, don't you?" Some months from now, at the Democratic Convention, I will see him wandering the outer corridors of the convention hall; as he walks around and around, he'll attract attention, a small crowd will follow him awhile and leave him for another crowd to attach itself, which will also soon leave him, having learned in the brief walk with him over the course of five minutes that he's a dead man. Out in the convention itself, as one losing contestant after another for this year's nomination is introduced to applause, Hart's name will not be mentioned once in four days. After a while, following him in the corridors of the convention hall, I'll abandon him too; and halfway through the convention, after the second day or so, he'll disappear altogether. Even in a world and century where a thousand images can live and die in the same moment, and resurrection therefore attends even the unlikeliest to be resurrected, Gary Hart is dead as dead gets. Before his second run in the same election he might well have still become president twelve years down the line, or at least secretary of state in someone else's government. Now that's impossible, and he's a free man at last.

• • •

To: Kiev, ul. Reznitskaya 13/15, Prokuratura USSR, Prokuroru OSIPENKO P.G., USSR. Dear Mr. Procurator: I am writing to respectfully call attention to the situation of Yury Badzyo, who has served nine years in prison and Siberian exile for his studies and writing. Badzyo is a researcher and scholar who was writing a study of the Ukraine when his work was confiscated and he was jailed in 1979. The work for which he received this punishment was never published or made public, and has by now undoubtedly been destroyed. I believe that in the eyes of the world Yury Badzyo is a true prisoner of conscience, having been imprisoned not for any act but for what he believes. I would urge that the remainder of his sentence be commuted as an affirmation of the Soviet Union's new policies of glasnost. I thank you for your serious attention to this matter.

There's light across this page I write, light through the trees that pass above me. The train now winds through a gully. The effect of the light through the trees along the top of the gully, hitting upon my page through my window, makes the writing so difficult that not only can I barely see what I've done, I can't imagine it either; the splatter of shadow swallows the memory of each word and alienates that memory from the next word I intend. What will Mr. Procurator make of this? How will I get Yury Badzyo out of Siberia if this light through the trees insists on blistering the meaning of what I say on his behalf? My letter fades in and out of the present. . . .

There's rain in the skies of Chicago . . . and *there's rain in the streets of Paris* remembers Sally *the day I come to him.* I find her sitting in the bar across from a club where I heard Son Seals singing only moments before. I cross the street in the rain and there she is in the bar called the Red Lion, they can't clear the shotglasses away from her fast enough, she's throwing the drinks back. *I've brought his daughter from America* she remembers *I am fourteen, Patsy not much younger. They had me bring her from America by way of England, we wait there for him to come meet us, he doesn't come.* . . .

He doesn't greet us either as we arrive in Paris, the servants say he's sick in the back room. Patsy goes to look for him. I wait,

the servants watch me. It will be two days before I see him. . . .
It's already crossed my mind I'm not in Virginia, that here I'm
free. I stand in his doorway. He's lying on the bed in the dark. His
face is in his hands, it's the headaches. I'm not calling him
Thomas yet but master or sir. I haven't said anything when he sits
up to look at me in the doorway. Who is it he says. Sally I say.
Sally? Does he remember me at all. I've changed in the time he's
been gone from home, Do I know you Sally? and I answer I'm
Betty Hemings' daughter, sir. I know I've changed. I look more
than fourteen, I've become of a color he has to remind himself I'm
black at all. He looks now in the light from the door behind me like
five years ago when his wife died and I was nine then standing
with the other servants and slaves in the room watching her on her
deathbed, and him by her, when she made him promise never to
marry again. But it may be that in that promise she bound him
to me, it may be that when she forbade any proper love after she
was gone she bound him thus to the improper love that frees the
darkness which lives in every saint. Now he peers from the ravages
of his racked head and sees in my changes who I am. I think I know
he wants me before he knows it. Yes I see Sally, he whispers and
lies back on the bed. After a moment he says Thank you for
bringing Patsy. Some day I'll take the pain from behind his eyes
and draw it up into me. But not tonight.

I don't know why I never saw that she's beautiful. I wouldn't
have looked at her twice if she hadn't called me by her lover's
name in the corridors of New Orleans. Later it would be called
to my attention, the fact that she's beautiful. But by then I've
nonetheless heard the sensual hush of her. Now she tries too
quickly to stand from her place there in the Red Lion: on the TV
above the bar is the news. She peers at it and sits down hard
where she's been. Some of the others look at her. She collects
something of herself and stands again, her balance wavering only
a moment; by will or history she would force herself into
sobriety. . . . Then I see she's crying. I help her outside. . . . I

expect no disengaged train coach to come rolling up Lincoln. I just walk her a block and suggest we should share a cab; I ask where she's staying. I hope she has an answer. If she does I don't hear it, and don't ask again. We get a cab, a black driver; she watches him with rage as he looks back at her in his rearview mirror. On Michigan Avenue she begins to cry again. *How much easier* I'm sure I hear her say *how much easier it would be, to be a slave who doesn't love her master.* It's full enough of anguish, the saying of it, that it might mean anything. Then she starts saying *Stop the cab.* We come to the part of Chicago near the river that's underground, little red saloons and an ancient Chicago they had to bury. The rain's coming down harder. It thunders against the street above us. I have this feeling she really has nowhere to go. *Stop the cab* she's saying and the driver pulls over, "Fine with me," he says and she gets out; and it's yet another taxi I've stopped in midjourney for Sally Hemings. She walks off into subterranean Chicago. "What about you," he says, "you getting out too?" No.

• • •

With the departure of Gary Hart from the presidential race, there's left only one other fullblown candidate of the nuclear imagination, and another touched by it. Both are Republicans, and neither is any more viable than Hart by the conclusion of Hart's candidacy, though as with Hart in 1984 there's a brief moment when the touched one has the presidency within reach. Robert Dole of Kansas, the minority leader of the United States Senate, lives with the abyss in him; it's not accurate, however, to argue that he's liberated by it. He has personalized the abyss and given it his memories, but it remains something to flee or awaken from. There's a great deal of talk of Dole's personal darkness; breaths were held in Dole's ascendancy, and knowing explanations are offered in his collapse. The best equipped of the candidates to be president, and one of the few who warrants the accolade of brilliance, he's also admired as a purely political animal when in fact, as events have come to show, he's not as fundamentally political as George Bush or Richard Gephardt. His sense of the absurd is too highly developed for him to be an entirely convincing political chameleon, and nothing inspires that sense of the absurd as politics itself. Twelve years ago, when Ronald Reagan challenged Gerald Ford for the Republican nomination and nearly took it from him, Dole was Ford's second choice for vice president, his first having been vetoed by the defeated Reagan as not being conservative enough. Years later Ford's first preference went on to become Reagan's chief of staff in the White House; his name was Howard Baker. Dole was put on Ford's ticket only with Reagan's approval; years later he has gone on to become something of a tacit Reagan critic, though by virtually any measure Dole himself is certainly a conservative Republican. Most political figures reach a point where they've so lost perspective they can't see the craziness of such turns of events. Dole not only positions himself accordingly but reminds people of the madness and the positioning with a wry relish. He likes to note that as a young man deciding on a political career in Kansas he made the "profound philosophical decision" to become a Republican when he looked around and noted there were more registered Republicans in his district than Democrats. Is any other major U.S. politician so naked and whimsical about his opportunism? It must make other politicians cringe. It also makes me trust Dole more than the other people running for the job. But as the incarnation of a literally wounded memory, Dole has come to disturb us. It's an entirely different sort of disturbance from that created by Gary Hart, but no less unsettling: even his flashes of humor suggest the abyss in him is something to be avenged, and we can't help but wonder if we'll be the ones to feel the vengeance. This is another reason I trust Dole, finding a naked face of rage more worthy of trust than a benevolent mask, particularly if behind the mask one perceives, as in the case of Bush, no face at all.

It's the night of the New Hampshire primary, and the abyss
in Robert Dole gapes. It gapes on television, in a notable snarl at
George Bush; Dole's not a man of delusion, and tonight he
understands he's lost not a primary but the presidency itself,
probably forever. The networks fill with voices discussing what
will happen next, and because Dole knows there is no Next,
because he's already made the fatal error of allowing himself to be
deluded by his pollsters, who've been telling him for forty-eight
hours that the primary, and by extension the Republican nomination, are his, he hates himself at this moment, and there's
nothing to check his contempt for the delusion. He probably feels
at this moment that he's the only person in the world who hasn't
lost his mind. When the network anchorman, with Bush sitting
at his side, asks Dole if there's anything he'd like to say to the vice
president, and when Dole remarks on how Bush has lied about
his record (in this particular case, regarding the issue of a tax
raise), he's actually saying, "I've lost the fucking presidency,
that's what I have to say. This is the day something irrevocable
happened to my life. This is the day my place in history became
immutably second-rate. What do I have to say? I'd as soon find
a tower somewhere, is what. A tower and one good gun, in a high
window, though my best arm is long since shattered. I'd as soon
have just enough in the finger of the hand on the end of my bad
arm to pull the fucking trigger and take any number of you
assholes with me. What else would you like to know? Why don't
you ask me how I'd like my political obituary phrased? We could
have a semantic discussion. Ask if I prefer cremation or the
donation of my body parts to whoever would want to have them,
such as they are. That's what I'd like to say to the vice president.
I'm *fucked!* That's what I'd like to say to Tom Brokaw. One good
tower. One good gun. This finger's just good enough for it. And
by the way, stop lying about my record." That's what he's saying
but he just leaves out everything up to the word "stop." Some
weeks later he's still campaigning, to the derision of smaller souls
who can see no point in anything but the winning and losing of

it. Sometimes, he actually tells someone, a body just twists in the wind until it begins to smell, and someone has to cut it down. It's my right to smell, is what Dole's challenge says: destiny has denied me too many times for me now to graciously forfeit the luxury of my stink. You want to cut me down? the challenge says: let the noise of your nerve match the flash of your blade. No one cuts me down; I'll twist until with one last shudder I revive long enough from the dead to do it myself. This is defiance in the face of political consensus, and the will of an animal possessed by something more than politics, which is the determination to find its own place and way to die.

Oddly, Dole's nova is even briefer than that of the only other candidate of the nuclear imagination, Pat Robertson; one would have expected it the other way around, given both Dole's stature and comparable stability, which are perhaps measured in the length and pitch of the dark that follows. It's only by stature Dole can go on dying as long as he does. Robertson, the leader of the Christian Right, dies on Super Tuesday in a mid-March blaze of nearly twenty state primaries and caucuses. The most significant contribution of Super Tuesday to the election process, if one can call it a contribution, is the way all nuance and implication are obliterated; nothing about it is subtle, for either the Republicans or the Democrats. All the mounting, cumulative claims on which campaigns are built are slashed loose on Super Tuesday: previously weak candidates who find success, like Albert Gore, can go on to survive loss after loss on the crest of that success, while previously successful candidates like Richard Gephardt, who seemed likely to contend all the way to the convention, are suddenly cut so low they can never recover. On Super Tuesday the campaign of Pat Robertson stops dead, after weeks of compounded wisdom that his power is on the rise. It stops dead for a number of reasons that include the scandals in the television evangelical industry, controversy over Robertson's service in the Korean War, and the array of what the press calls funny facts, a euphemism that came into favor during Ronald Reagan's rise for what we novelists call fiction and you civilians call lies. From Robertson, these funny facts have a quality that verges on the breathtaking. One can't consider them a candidate's miscalculations exactly, as though they've undone what would otherwise have been a successful campaign; rather they're born of the very nihilism of Robertson's vision. Robertson's lies have both audacity and imagination; like Adolf Hitler pursuing the chancellorship of Germany, Robertson will take the truth, turn it inside out and hurl it back at those who question it, such as his furious charge that anyone calling him a television evangelist is a religious bigot. Not only does he cast himself as the victim in such an exchange, but the charge flies in the face of miles of television footage documenting his evangelical career over the course of twenty years and disorients everyone and means to transform truth itself by sheer will and gall. Thus, like Hitler, Robertson's always saying things so startling they're guaranteed to dominate the discussion and leave his opponents unsure how to respond: his contentions, for instance, that he's known for years the location of American hostages in Iran, or that George Bush was really behind the scandal involving another television evangelist, Jimmy Swaggart. The press apparently assumes that Robertson's reinvention is on too large a scale to indicate the instability of Gary Hart's more trivial selfalterations. Though this leads into a complicated discussion of just what is crazy, Robertson is probably not a madman any more than Hitler in the early years of his career; on the other hand, the madness that overtook Hitler later clearly had its seeds in him all along. These are the seeds of nihilism, as well as an attendant imagination that's liberated by the abyss, infused by the blood of an armageddon with no god.

If Robertson actually believed in a god he wouldn't exploit God so recklessly. His are the motions of a man sure of the void, and therefore free to fill the void with his own image, for those who follow him. It would not only be unfair to accuse Robertson's followers of such a nihilism but would as well misunderstand the dynamics of his political pull. Most of Hitler's followers, not the inner circle but those among the masses, weren't nihilists either; fascism by emotional definition demands a nihilistic leader and followers who, far from nihilism, hurt with a hungry faith. As opposed to people for whom religion reinforces their sense of themselves and enlightens their place in the universe, the core of Robertson's followers are fascists for Jesus. I don't use the word fascist indulgently in the manner of those in the New Left who since the 1960s have called everyone from Hubert Humphrey rightward a fascist. Robertson's followers can legitimately be called fascists because of their palpable disgust with democratic pluralism and their dedication to replacing that pluralism with a single neomythic figure to whom they submit not simply their wills or their doubts but the blankness inside them that causes them so much pain. Before that pain the consequences of the Bill of Rights are only threatening and fearful. Much of Robertson's campaign is predicated on moral issues that neither the government nor the presidency have anything to do with; when young women with their babies in their arms file out of Robertson rallies speaking sincerely of the need for a president who will bring morality back into the private lives of the people in this country, it's difficult to know how it is they suppose the president will do this. Clearly the premise of Robertson's moral campaign presumes one of two things: that people do not understand the presidency, the Constitution or the Bill of Rights; or that they do understand them and their intention is to change them. Theirs is the clear conviction that America was meant to be a Christian country rather than one where Christians are free to be Christians and non-Christians free to be non-Christians.

In the eyes of many of those supporting Pat Robertson is a hate as cold and sharp as a diamond. It curdles the words of Jesus' love which they profess; they look to Jesus' return with a rapturous anticipatory relish for the pain and suffering and damnation it will bring to the unsaved. Their actual loathing of Jesus precedes every announcement of dedication; as it happens, Jesus is already back, and they despise him. I saw him just the other day. It's April in New York; I saw him on the Bowery. I believe he was tying the cord that bulged the vein of the junkie sending himself to heroin heaven; afterward Jesus took that smacksotted corpse to his chest and smiled deeply with tragic dismay. Saw him in the West Hollywood clinic in October with the dying homosexual, gathering up the flesh that fell away from the sinner like leaves beneath autumn rain; he smiled the same way. Jesus doesn't hang out with a lot of Republicans. Most of them walk over him on the sidewalk where he sleeps in a box, eating garbage. They'd as soon clean Jesus out of their lives. They love his divinity and spit on his humanity, which counted for more than his divinity ever did. They exalt a morality they claim to have derived from him, and the malice of it mitigates their own wounds and misunderstanding; those who follow this malice are afflicted by a culture that baffles them. Some of them have nothing in life but Pat Robertson, who knows that empires are built on the lies that fools believe. In the process, in the flush of a desperate holiness that people clutch to when their own humanity is monstrous to them, that humanity becomes monstrous indeed; it says everything about this monstrous vision of humanity that Jimmy Swaggart's encounter with a prostitute was somehow less sinful in the eyes of the faithful because he only watched her do obscene things rather than actually commit something human like make love to her. The matrons of the Christian Right would rather risk children dying of a sexually transmitted plague than have them learn about it before it suits their "values." What genre of loathing makes the human spirit so mean? It's enough to wake you up in the night. It's enough to make you call out in the night the name of the Jesus whose humanity you love even as you doubt his divinity, that he'd take the whip to those who exploit his name for political power as he took it to those who exploited the name of the God he loved for the sake of a profit. But then in calling out such a thing you're left to wonder about the meanness in your own spirit. In the end Jesus didn't need a whip. In the end he was all over the South, he and Sally Hemings, counting ballots with cruelly disfigured hands, feeling the balm of an evinced collective wisdom that sent Pat Robertson to defeat.

• • •

There are rumors in the countryside, I hear them. Even as some try to protect me from them I hear them. I don't need this protection. I am a liar if I pretend to feel shame. I feel no shame. I am a liar if I pretend I feel no pride that I am the great man's slave and mistress. I rule his land with him, his house. I bear his children, sons that bear his face, daughters that bear mine, I bore the latest not fourteen months back. When the rumors began I denied nothing, more than this neither did he, he has not denied me. His white love washes the black womb of me still, his old white love. I have been his lover now fifteen years. He is more than threescore in years, I am less than half that. More than half the life I've lived I've lived as the prisoner of his ownership but also the keeper of the beast in him, the beast that any saint has living in him, so that he might learn to see in the dark. . . . Russell the coachman whispers to me of freedom. But I left that behind in Paris when we returned to Virginia, I left that behind in the streets when the people of Paris yanked the prison walls down to rubble. . . . I hear it. I hear the sound of that, in the way that the fire I see burns of the freedom forsaken; I don't wish to hear or see any of it. I don't want to consider my forsaken freedom or the other destiny of this country I perhaps abandoned with it. Russell, whip the horses faster. Alexandria is still a twilight away.

Russell stops the coach at an inn. I keep the curtains closed and remain in the coach. I am light enough to be presumed not a negro but my face is rumored all over the countryside from home to the capitol. Russell a slave himself seethes at being my slave, the slave of another slave. Also, I can see how he wants me. I've seen it from the plantation porch, last night he said to me Get your children and I'll take the lot of you up north and from America. But they're Thomas' children too, I said back. That's not the real reason, Russell said; and he's right. So Russell seethes at everything since the night six weeks ago I kissed him, I should not have done it. I don't love Russell but he's young and beautiful and negro and just once I wanted to kiss a man who was not old and forlorn and white, just once I wanted a man who was not great, a man neither saint nor with inside him the beast of a saint. There's a knock on the carriage door and I hear Russell's voice and open the door. Behind him I can see the innkeeper's wife in the door of the inn, peering curiously at the carriage. Russell hands me a plate of food. When the horses are rested we'll be on our way, he says angrily. The innkeeper's wife prepared a meal for you, he adds; she stands in the doorway to make sure it's eaten by a fine lady in a carriage and not no nigger. There's nothing I can say to Russell to soften him short of offering to flee with him to Canada, and he knows that's impossible now having left the children at Monticello. Have some of my food Russell, I say looking over his shoulder at the woman in the door, I can't eat it all. But there isn't a chance he'll eat some of my food. When the horses are rested, he repeats. He slams the door shut. . . .

We are in Alexandria past dark. . . . Arrangements have been made. At the back of the boardinghouse Russell pulls the coach to a stop and the housekeeper opens the door for me. Russell nearly wrestles the door from him, the shock on the housekeeper's face is that of a man who's seen something supernatural. For a moment I believe the keeper will raise his rod to Russell's back. Russell's mood is frightening and murderous. I step from the coach between them. I ask Russell to unhitch the horses and take them to the stable. He radiates rage. The housekeeper's wife leads me into the back service area of the house while the keeper stands watching Russell and the horses. The keeper's wife and I ascend the backstairs to a small suite on the top floor. From the window here I can see the shabby lights of the new capitol of the country across the swamp, small flimsy shelters and a half-finished structure for the government and the long flat palisades not unlike those Thomas and I knew in Paris. He has built his own Paris here amid the mud and slop and pestilence. Russell brings up my trunk. When the keeper tells him that he will sleep in the stable I am afraid for my control of matters here, I'm afraid of what Russell's capable of at this moment. I know the keeper wants to beat him. He is still affronted by the business with the carriage door. I am still enough of a slave and enough of a black to recognize the white master who would beat the black slave. He will sleep in quarters in the back of the house, I say to the keeper, this is the president's man. The keeper looks at me. He looks back at Russell. Perhaps the president, the keeper says, will give you the thrashing that's in order. The president does not thrash his slaves, I say, please find him comfortable quarters in the back of the house. It does not entirely soothe Russell that I must interject myself here, though he is not insulted when I say This is the president's man. I don't believe he wants to feel any honor of it though, in the way I feel the honor of those who look at me and say with their eyes though not their tongues, This is the president's whore.

I am the president's whore. I am a liar if I pretend I feel no honor of it. It's what I chose to be in Paris, where it was my choice to stay and live a free woman instead. He was forlorn in the five years since his wife's death, he was forlorn in the wake of his broken forbidden affairs in Paris. Let it be said he promised nothing to me he would not deliver. I won't free you in America, he told me then, should you return to America with me. I can't promise I will. I can't promise I would ever marry you even if I *could, he said, I am now old enough to know which ideals I can never live up to. He first took me only weeks before my fifteenth birthday, he had me in a beastly way and I told him this. You're a beast, I said to him. And when I said it to him, I freed the darkness in him that his life of the mind had left locked up so long. He mounted me then as a man who mounts his own spirit, in order to remind it of ravenous appetites it has pretended to disbelieve. So there was nothing in it for him to take me back to America a free woman, there was nothing in it for him to take me anywhere but where I would be his slave and whore. He had felt the dark ferocious pleasure of the beast and liked it; in the moment I released the beast in him and he shot the beast back into me his dreams completed themselves; and the desires he had neglected, the power he had turned away from, flooded him as he flooded me: he became a ruler then. He did not talk of freeing the slaves anymore as he had so passionately when he was younger. He did not turn away from the political designs others fashioned for him, and the destiny of those designs that would make him what he now is. The beast of him met the saint of him, and his dream thus became the act. As his slave I have both of him, the beast and the saint, whereas a free whore or a free wife would have only one or the other.*

I fall asleep for a while; when I wake the candle has gone out. It must be past midnight. I fall asleep again and wake to the sound on the stairs. For a moment I almost say it, when he's in the doorway, I almost say Russell. I have been asleep and dreaming. I almost say Russell, but then I know it's not Russell, he turns in the door to those on the stairs behind him, speaks softly not out of deference to my sleep but because he never speaks but softly. The keeper and his wife seem confounded by him as others are always confounded by him, this vagabond ruler in his rags, towering tall enough he must slouch to miss the ceiling. The door closes. He speaks to me. I'll pretend to be asleep a while longer. After he's asleep I find myself fully awake, the light of the far capitol through

*the window; and in the pit of his sleep I touch myself, and have a
vision. . . .*

• • •

In mid-April I'm in New York, staying in a hotel on West 81st
Street across from the Museum of Natural History. The hotel's
run by Germans and everyone in the hotel is German except me.
I hear German in the elevators and on the stairs, German maids
bark at me in the hallways. Sometimes everyone stops talking
when I walk into the lobby. My first room in this hotel has a
telephone that doesn't work, so I'm moved to a suite on one of
the top floors. I have a bedroom, living room, bathroom and
kitchen. I wander from room to room, and everything I wish to
do, whether it's watching TV or sleeping, I have to do in different
rooms. The electricity's enormous. I thought I'd leave it somewhere in the country behind me; I left Los Angeles slapping
everything metal with which I came into contact. I slapped my
way across the United States. Chicago was electric-casual, the
country electric-friendly. My suite in this German hotel on West
81st Street in New York City is electric-hostile; every inch of it
conspires to fry me with an austere teutonic glee. It becomes best
just to leave the TV on all the time at the appropriate volume.
The news is all about the primary which is several days away.
The three Democratic contenders flee back and forth across the
city and my television screen in electric waves, twenty-four hours
a day.

The primary's the first political manifestation in memory of
the kind of importance New York always assumes belongs to it as
a matter of course. Should the primary be won by the governor
of Massachusetts, Michael Dukakis, and won in some kind of
convincing manner, he'll almost certainly be the nominee of the
party in the summer. Should he lose, or win only barely, the
nominee will probably be the governor of New York; and the
governor of New York, Mario Cuomo, appears to maneuver
accordingly. Cuomo can be taken at face value as not wanting to

run for the nomination, and there seems no chance at all he'd enter the race before the Democratic Convention in Atlanta; this doesn't mean he'd be loath to accept a nomination delivered to him by the party with a minimum of fuss and muss. In the meantime there's the mayor of New York City, who hates the governor and would therefore love to see him president of a foreign country like the United States. Thus the mayor has endorsed the senator from Tennessee, Albert Gore. On TV there's news footage of the two on streetcorners trying to shake the hands of people who walk by insulting them. New Yorkers are clearly cracking under the strain of all this importance they've claimed for themselves so long but which they've always intuitively understood is unwarranted; now they have to live up to it, and the resulting spectacle isn't pretty. I walk up and down the street and see it in their eyes, all of them saying to themselves, You mean *we're* picking the next president of the United States? They can't help feeling contempt for a situation that would actually allow them to make such a choice. The mayor of the city, Koch, is all that's angry and arrogant about New York wound up so tight that a loose end is bound to burst free, some ugly bit of rhetoric, usually about Jews and blacks; the guy can't put a lid on it. When you'd thought nothing could shame Al Gore, he actually looks ashamed on TV; he's mortified by Koch. At rallies all over the city on the weekend before the primary, the people of New York seem on the verge of a mass collective breakdown; it's a cry for help, silent and desperate. Please, please, it goes, take this importance away from us, we can't stand it. And as they know Koch is Their New Yorker through and through, so too they scream down his name whenever it comes up, no matter who they may be for; when the energy level of a rally ebbs, the speaker can always count on raising it back up again with one word: Koch. The crowd roars blackly at the sound of it. They hate the guy for how he embodies them. The day following the primary you can already read his political obituaries.

The weather may be a factor in the primary, affecting the

turnout and therefore altering the chances of this candidate or that. In fact, New York's glorious this week, marred by rain only the day before the vote. That night I have a drink with a magazine editor in a bar near Columbus Circle. A large screen over the bar broadcasts a ball game, the Mets I guess, who've been winning of late. People in the city talk of nothing, including the primary, as much as these fucking Mets. In the town where I come from we have a sport for grownups called basketball, but I suppose it's OK with me that New York has its nice little baseball games. I suppose it's also OK with me six months from now when the L.A. baseball team thrashes these Mets good. After the magazine editor leaves I watch the game for a while and then head up Columbus and hit another bar on the way, since I'm researching the mood of the city. Getting its pulse and all that. The game's still going in this other bar, and afterward comes the news, more campaign updates, a quasidebate between the candidates, more yammer from the mayor, meanwhile a tipsy blond woman plays Sixties songs on the jukebox and choogles frantically out of rhythm. Then she has another drink. A couple of guys in suits stand around. I have my last drink for the evening as an older woman on the eleven o'clock news is explaining that her vote tomorrow will be more against the mayor than any of the actual candidates: "I think he's just . . . lost his mind," she says very quietly. The blond woman sits two seats away yelling at me, "Purple haze! Is in my brain!" She says over and over, angrily, "I was *there*, I was there man. I was a child of the Sixties." When I get up to leave, her voice changes and becomes coy. "Hey you." I've seen her before, in the hotel elevator maybe.

What happens next, I can't say for sure. There's no telling *what* they've been serving in this bar, there's no telling *what* is in the air in New York this spring. But a year from now some perverse part of me may prefer to remember it like this:

I go back to the hotel, I go up to my room, I ground myself, I turn channels, I drink soda, I take Tylenol, I drink more soda,

I take off my shirt, I wander around the suite, in this room and that, I turn on the faucet in the bathroom, I brush my teeth, I walk around the suite some more before I wash my face, I should call my wife, I should call all the campaign headquarters and find out where the various primary-night parties will be when the vote comes in, I wash my face, I think I can handle some more soda, I look from my bedroom window, I look from my living-room window, I adjust the heat, I go back to the bathroom, I decide to take a shower, I take off my clothes and get in the shower for a few minutes, I think I hear my phone ringing but it's coming through my bathroom window from the window of another suite, I get out of the shower, I dry off, I wrap a towel around me and go in to watch the TV some more and there in the middle of the living room is the blond child of the Sixties from the bar.

For a moment I can't say anything and then I'm sputtering something even I don't understand. She's just standing in the middle of my suite with her eyes closed. In two seconds she'll pass out here and I'll have this woman lying on my floor. I just want to grab her and push her out my door but I can't do that, she'll collapse any moment. She gestures at me when I talk, waving away whatever it is I have to say. I know in a moment the phone's going to ring and it's going to be Astrid and it's going to be apparent to her from my voice that a drunken blond woman from a bar is lying on the floor of my suite. I'm in a panic to get this woman out of here before the phone rings. I'm trying to remember where I've seen her before, I'm thinking she's familiar because maybe I saw her come out of one suite or another on my floor sometime in the last few days; she's just wandered into my room by mistake. When I stop trying to say whatever it is I've been trying to say, there's another moment of silence. "You're gonna cry! Ninety-six tears!" she says then, in the still of the suite. "You gonna cry, cry cry cry! Night and day! ninety-six tears. . . ." Now if my wife calls at this moment she'll not only hear in my voice how there's this woman in my suite, but she'll actually hear the woman in the background singing a 1966 song by ? and the Mysterians. I take her by the shoulders and move her toward the door, when someone knocks on the door.

We both stand there in the middle of the suite watching the door now. She's sobered up some, though she keeps narrowing her eyes as though trying to get the door into better focus. We both stand there awhile waiting for whoever's at the door to leave, but the knocking continues and sounds angrier by the moment. Then there's a man's voice on the other side, with a slight Southern accent, and now the woman's quite sober, she's much better focused on the door, and in her face I can see her going back and forth between hysteria and defiance; on the other side of the door he speaks again. She backs away from the sound of his voice. I understand now I have a problem here. I head for the door to attach the chain when the knob begins to turn. As the knob turns the woman scatters toward my bathroom to hide and I make a crazy dash to the bedroom where I throw myself beneath the covers of my bed. The lights are blazing away in the living room along with the television, and when I hear someone in the doorway, as I'm pretending to sleep, the telephone on the table beside me begins to ring. I just lie there while it goes on ringing.

The guy in the doorway bends down by my bed. His face is about two inches from mine. He's waiting for me to open my eyes: the phone has rung about six times now. "Ring ring," the guy says. I open my eyes and we're looking at each other; I can't make him out that well in the dark, but I know from the news on the TV he's had a hard day. "The telephone," he drawls, on about the ninth ring. I still don't answer, I just lie there under the covers. When the telephone stops the guy says, "Where's my wife," and then, "I know my wife is here, I have *friends*." I remember the guys in the bar dressed in suits.

"I've had nothing to do with her," I finally tell him. I don't even like your wife, I want to tell him. . . . The guy's still inches from my face. "I could speak to the manager of the hotel," I say, "you're in my room."

"Yes," the guy says, "you could speak to the manager of the hotel. Sure. How do you suppose I got in here? I have connections in this town." I guess he means the mayor. I guess after hanging around streetcorners all day with the mayor he figures he ought to at least get to throw his name around for all the embarrassment it's caused him. I can sense the man's tense; I don't want to push him. "What's your name," he says. I tell him. "What do you do," he says; I tell him. He asks me what I've written and I tell him a couple of books and he asks the names of the books and I tell him. "I've never heard of those books," he says. "In fact, I've never heard of you. How old are you anyway." I tell him thirty-eight. He's delighted by this, this is exactly the sort of answer that was almost too much to hope for. "I just turned forty a week ago," he says, "forty years old. That's two years older than you. Do you know what I'm going to be someday?" he says. President of the United States, I'm thinking to myself. "President of the United States," he says. I can see him nodding in the dark. "You're a writer no one's ever heard of and I'm two years older than you, probably younger than some of your *best friends*, and someday I'm going to be president of the United States. That's the difference, isn't it. Between you and me. Between you and me and your best friends. It may not be this year. It may be four or eight or twelve years down the road. At *our* age, Mr. Writer, I've got another *seven* elections to do it in. You know, I may make it in the year 2016. When you're still a writer no one's heard of picking up other men's wives in cheap Central Park hotels. How about that. Do you know *why* we're different?" Maybe she's listening to all this, hiding in the bathroom; maybe she hears all of it, maybe it makes her feel like the first time he told it to her. "We're different because I made the decision," he explains, there in the dark at my bedside, "I made the decision when I was six that I'd be president. Because at six I found in myself the ambition and hunger for as much power as the human race finds fit to bestow on a single person, including the power to destroy that race. From the time I was six nothing meant as much to me. Gephardt was, I don't know, probably *ten* when he made such a decision. Maybe he was already into *puberty*. That's the difference between me and him. Nothing can stop someone who makes a decision like that when he's six. I was bred for it. I went to the best schools. A senator's son with all the connections. And of course it hasn't hurt that I happen to be a man for whom sheer ambition is justification in itself, not only justification enough but the sort of justification to which something like authenticity would only be an obstacle. How can you stop me? I'm a *favorite*. I was made for words like bright and young and articulate and attractive, I was made for the words of magazine writers. Magazine editors take me under their wings. They endorse me on their covers and when I fail they write mystified articles about how it must be that people just don't know how really articulate I am. How really attractive. What a fine sense of humor I have, and how I can talk about hip things like whether the Beatles were better than the Rolling Stones. The Beatles were *always* better than the Rolling Stones. That's the difference between you and me. There was probably a time when you thought the Rolling Stones were better, didn't you. I never had such a time, that's the difference. Any halfway contemplative individual would, in the darkest moments when he knows what he's capable of, at least once in his or her life consider the possibility that the Rolling Stones were better, but I never had such a moment. So next time the magazine editors will still be in my corner. They've invested their own thwarted futures in me, I'm the dashing young president all of them once wanted to be. Maybe even you too. And sooner or later they'll put me over. Sooner or later people will forget my wife's idiotic campaign against rock and roll, or will be converted to it. We'll *all* know that the Beatles were *always* better than the Rolling Stones. The senators I've offended, obsolete coots, they'll be discarded by the wayside. Because in the end nothing obstructs a pure ambition that's had years to construct itself, adding the finishing touches, that's had years to acquire a sheen to its falseness. Mr. Writer. Mr. Writer with two books nobody's heard of. Because in the end they'll notice, not consciously perhaps but at some level of perception, how much I look like a younger version of the current president. Have you noticed that? Thirty-eight and here you are. In this shabby little hotel with my pudgy wife, what, she's probably hiding in the *bathroom* or something. Forget it. She and I, we're a *couple*." He's getting a little worked up. "I'm, uh . . . I'm feeling a little, uh. . . ." He can't bring himself to say it. Down inside him somewhere, at this moment, he likes the Rolling Stones better. "I . . ." He's capable of anything at this moment; at this moment, he's Richard Nixon from the right side of the tracks. He's standing now, off his knees from my bedside, and he could be mumbling at anyone. He keeps talking about the next time, he keeps talking about magazine editors who'll put him over. He leaves the room, I can't tell if he's heading for the bathroom; maybe, if she was using her head, she slipped out in the middle of all that. Maybe she's heard it often enough she knows he's got at least another ten minutes of it in him; probably at such moments you could set the guy on fire and he'd never notice. "Gephardt must have been . . . I'll bet he was at least *twelve* before it ever even *occurred* to him. . . ." He's a bit out there now, I can tell. Right now he's getting so far out as to be even harmless. Tomorrow he'll have it together again when the returns come in and they're disastrous. He'll pull it together and give a magnanimous concession speech. Two days after that he'll withdraw from the race completely and give another magnanimous speech. He'll do his damnedest impersonation of grace and humility in defeat; he'll start mending fences right away. At some point in the evening the drone of him from the other room is just too much and I fall asleep, realizing it somewhere in the back of my mind, hoping he just closes the door behind him.

• • •

When the primary is over, the man who may be president, Michael Dukakis, has taken New York State, while in defiance of both the mayor and his candidate, the man who will not be president has taken New York City. Four years ago I was standing in the back of San Francisco's Moscone Center when Jesse Jackson addressed the convention of the Democratic Party. The speech he gave that Tuesday night has since become legendary, and perhaps there's not much point here in noting that it was not in fact a really great speech. It was, rather, a fair speech with two great moments, in a great and momentous context. The first of these moments was Jackson's confession, the second Jackson's plea. Together the two electrified the convention that night, and launched Jackson toward the 1988 election. If you go back and watch a tape of the 1984 speech you may be startled to hear how many of the themes of the election to come four years later are born in it, or how many find their fullest life and greatest exposure: the patchwork-quilt metaphor of a multicolored American community, the ringing challenge of moving from racial battleground to economic commonground to moral higherground. These may have been things Jackson said before the Moscone Center speech but the Moscone Center speech is significant for how a shifting audience gave those themes new weight and power. Because only in retrospect is it now clear, in a way it wasn't then, how Jackson was sending his address over his constituency in the convention hall—which then was nearly all black—to a new constituency. It's forgotten, for instance, that a lot of blacks in the Moscone Center that Tuesday night in 1984 weren't all that thrilled with Jackson's speech. It had been eagerly awaited after a series of weeks in which both Jackson and his supporters felt Jackson had not been treated as he deserved, which is to say as one of the party's leading spokesmen. His delegate strength did not represent his popular strength in the primaries, and Walter Mondale had not included Jackson in deliberations about most of the important issues, the selection of

the vice-presidential nominee and party chairman among them.
As well, there were deep divisions among blacks over Mondale
and Jackson themselves, and over Jackson's minority planks to
the platform, which were all beaten in resounding fashion on the
very afternoon of the evening Jackson was to speak. Blacks were
booing Atlanta mayor Andrew Young, once a civil-rights hero
who would go on to host the party convention in his own city
four years later; and in caucus they actually booed Coretta Scott
King as well, which is a little like Catholics hurling tomatoes at
the Virgin Mary. Finally there were all the crises of Jackson's
own creation: his relationship with hatemonger Louis Farrakhan,
whom Jackson renounced only when he was about to be kicked
out of the convention; and his comments about Jews which were
stupid at best and bigoted at worst. When Jackson did speak that
night, a number of delegates walked out.

The reason many blacks weren't happy with Jackson's
speech was that he chose to speak not to his dissatisfactions, and
therefore theirs, but rather to his redemption. In that way he
spoke over his constituency, to his next constituency, though
most of the commentators that night and the next morning told
it the other way—a speech by Jesse to make the blacks in the hall
happy. A number of blacks were chagrined by what Jackson had
to say; but Jackson, whose political instincts may be as good as
anyone's in the country, understood at some level, even as his
ego may not have allowed him to admit it, that for someone who
had built his campaign on what he called moral imperatives, he
had thus sabotaged the logic and justification of that campaign
with his own anti-Semitism. It was like Richard Nixon making
political hay out of the issue of law and order: he was the last
person who could afford the lawlessness of Watergate. Jackson
was the last person who could afford the appearance of intolerance. The ace up Jackson's sleeve was that the people in the
Moscone Center that night wanted to believe him; they weren't
impervious to his charisma or the devotion of his people in the

hall, or whatever influence, presumably major, he might have in delivering some five to seven Southern states to Mondale in November, not to mention industrial states in the Northeast. That none of this came to pass will not mitigate his influence at this year's convention; rather, Jackson relentlessly reminds the party of his role in helping it recapture the Senate in 1986. I remember four years ago the demonstration for Jackson in the convention hall being oddly muted, its fervor laced with the strychnine of uncertainty, and that he spoke for nearly eight minutes without any reaction at all, appealing to delegates to cast their vote for him on the first ballot as a matter of conscience. When he said he would be proud to support Mondale in the election, the tension flew out of the room; and then Jackson, whose sense of timing had already developed to the transcendent, offered one of the most astonishing mea culpas ever made by a major political figure over national television, the kind of apology that might have saved Nixon had he been shrewd or sincere enough to give it. Jackson didn't just repent, he asked forgiveness, and the masterstroke of the convention was the line "Be patient, God is not finished with me yet." None of us could quite believe what we'd heard. Jackson finessed his dilemma by saying that he was an instrument of God, and that God had been less than hasty in the matter of making Jesse Jackson perfect. If everyone would just give Him a little more time, God would get it right, eventually. Who was going to refuse such a request? Who was going to turn down an appeal to give God a little more time? By begging the crowd to stick with him, Jackson had asked us to stick with God.

It was in this flash of messianic contrition that the Jackson campaign of 1988 was born. It was a contrition that wouldn't entirely placate Jews, it was a contrition that was bound to offend blacks for whom contrition is mortification. Nonetheless it was contrition that was not really addressed to either Jews or blacks but to the new American constituency that loomed before

Jackson as far back as 1984; whether he saw it or not it loomed in his understanding of America's political reality, which is to say the political reality of the illusory identity of the United States. Over the four years to come Jackson would keep his cool with the Jews, more or less, betraying only impatience on occasion, impatience with the question of anti-Semitism as it continued to hound him, long after Jackson in his own mind had spoken to the question with a confession unlike any ever made by a major political figure, and one that many blacks had to resent, since one is hard-pressed to remember a white figure ever making such a confession to blacks. And what I've noted most recently in Jackson is that the rage in his eyes is gone: forty-eight hours before the 1988 New York primary Jackson spent the day in New York City, beginning with a walk across a bridge that's been closed because it's falling apart; that afternoon there was a rally on the Upper West Side at 72nd and Amsterdam. The crowd was a mix of blacks and white yuppies; Jackson was four hours late. But we waited the four hours and when he bounded to the stage there was a warm light in his face I hadn't seen four years ago; he was also bulkier, in a blue raincoat, part of it his own new bulk and part the bulletproof vest he wore, but the effect at any rate was to make him almost jolly. Jackson had been transformed. As with all great political con men, as with Ronald Reagan himself, Jackson's own performance of Jesse Jackson has come to transform him; I don't see how it could have been otherwise. Because he *has* found, to some extent, his new constituency; and though it might not be a constituency to take him to the White House this year or four years or eight years from now, it's nonetheless something beyond Jackson's own wildest expectations: whites turning out twenty-five, thirty, thirty-five percent to support him in Vermont, Wisconsin, the wildest, most unimaginable places a small black boy in Greenville, South Carolina, might ever have once considered. Now there were white faces here to greet him and cheer for him; and the cynic in him may have held contempt for us, disbelieving us, assuming we were there only to congratulate ourselves for our liberalism, or to congratulate ourselves for having been suckered by him: there is a part of Jesse Jackson that once played us for suckers. Except that Jesse Jackson has suckered himself. On the stand he gives the usual speech, he leads the crowd in the same call-and-response, but he has two moments I'm not sure he was capable of four years ago. The first is ironic, when he talks about the next day's rally to be held in Harlem: "Five-thirty tomorrow afternoon," he smiles to the white audience, "it'll still be light, you'll be OK," and then he adds, "when it gets dark it won't matter anyway, because we all look the same in the dark." He's taunting our fears but it's not mean, he's getting us to laugh at them, we almost believe we could all go up to Harlem tomorrow and hang out and it would be all right. Then he picks up a newspaper, I think it's the *Post*, and the headline says the primary is too close to call, and a number of speakers on the stand this evening have brandished this headline before us, the hope that Jesse Jackson can win the primary; but now Jackson barely makes note of it. He mentions it only briefly and then begins thumbing to the back pages of the *Post*. "There's a story here about child abuse," he says, back on page eight; and maybe it's all a show, maybe Jackson doesn't really care about the story on page eight, or maybe he knows that the headline about the primary being close is in fact a death sentence for his chances, in the way his victory in the Michigan caucus doomed his chances in Wisconsin, scaring a whole new sector of the electorate into turning out and voting for Dukakis. But it doesn't seem that way, it seems real, Jackson's concern about this story on page eight and child abuse.

Jackson's loss in New York is the end for him this year. A month and a half later he fights valiantly in California, in a primary held almost twenty years to the day after Robert Kennedy was killed in the Ambassador Hotel in Los Angeles; on the news reports Jackson can barely speak. His voice is gone, his hope mangled. There are any number of good and hardheaded reasons to support Dukakis, not the least of which being that a win in the California primary might reinforce his position in the November election; also, Dukakis might be a better president than Jackson. But it doesn't seem, on the twentieth anniversary of Kennedy's death, that Jackson deserves to lose so badly.

Now it's Leap Summer. I'm riding the train called the Crescent down from New York through Washington, down from Washington through the South. This train of liars, riding through the black hole of the land's dream: we roar across its purgatory in a gale of fire. It's the summer God laughs at America's faith. The ground outside my window is a hundred and forty degrees. The small black rivers outside my window have risen in black steam and left their boats in black mud. Throughout the South people turn on their faucets to seawater that has crept inland to the reservoirs. It's a United States without borders, as I've seen from Chicago through Pennsylvania, the small houses whose yards run to the streets, streets without curbs or sidewalks, and now in the drought and heat the United States without borders is covered with thirsty dust and now the United States I see from my window is nothing but houses in a dust through which shows only on occasion the black of streets, like still dead pools. In the train stations Christmas music is played over the speakers, so as to fool us. Birds fly erratically, unsure whether the sky is hotter than the ground. Dusty brown neighborhoods with dead black asphalt ponds and flocks of birds frantically searching along the streets for some place God has not abandoned. Lone navajo magicians are hired to dance beneath the empty skies. In Brownsville, Texas, nethersouthernpoint of the United States, in a country where only east and west understand civilization and only north and south understand the void, a sudden rainstorm appears, to drop six inches in two hours with a force literally powerful enough to collapse a department store; one person dies for every inch. People rush from the heat in panic to the beaches where they find small fields of old hypodermic needles and vials of plague blood growing lethal from the sand; the seas are awash with the disposed debris of hospital patients. Dolphins beach on the shores dying of chemical burns. Whole rivers are so excremental they don't even show up on weather-satellite photos anymore as rivers. We don't deserve God. We've fouled what he gave us and so he goes away. He deserts us like the master who deserts in disgust the pet who fouls its own nest, knowing something about the animal is unnatural. On the eve of July Fourth we can watch our celebration in the skies, a punctured airplane of Islam over the banks of Persia, a ghastly faithless firecracker, Iranians slipping out one by one. Americans quarrel for weeks over whether we should admit regretting this, assuming we do. This is what the faith of Ronald Reagan's U.S.A. was bound to come to, a faith that needed no act of redemption, only reclaimed innocence as though the soul never sees the sun go down at all. Faith is reclaimed here simply by suffering enough, and snapping oneself out of it: America's new faith is in faith itself, like an extension of Roosevelt's axiom about fear. We have come to worship the ritual of worship. The currency of our modern faith has no real reserves, it's not based on anything that stands the scrutiny of reason or ethics. On every side of any issue we may opt for the solutions of blind faith, whether they're elephantine defense budgets or phony nuclear freezes, even as these solutions have no application to anything that resembles lessons of doubt. We've chosen to forget the lessons altogether. It's a national policy that doubt is for wimps. If it is the most doubt-ridden issue of the day, having to do with the very nature of the human soul and at what point it weds itself to biological entity, it will nonetheless find its happy visceral expression reduced to a matter of "choice" on the one hand and "murder" on the other. It's not the American way to accommodate the issue's doubts except to try and seize their benefit, whether on behalf of women's bodies or the unborn. We've so dazzled ourselves with our faith in blind faith, we've so persuaded ourselves of some American dawn, that we haven't noticed how the dark night goes on. If you met someone wandering around at three in the morning who thought the sun was shining, you might consider it a remarkable act of faith. But you might also think he was asleep. You might even think he was crazy.

Down on the Crescent then through the Leap South, caught in twenty-four hours of leap sun that never end: down through Alexandria and Manassas and Culpeper, Charlottesville and Lynchburg, Greensboro and Gastonia and Greenville. Where America was born of a holocaustic power and hope, and deserted itself almost in the same breath, finding nothing was possible in the heat of the country and its idea but for conscience to concede to sanity, only to be left with the result of dark madness. As someone who betrays his ideals on a daily basis, I know this even having never known it. The dust of the drought sheathes the train window, children's carts waste in summer ash, snakes lie in blistered fragments on the rails that are wet with steely summershimmer. Down into the hole of America, preGod and postChaos, reports filter in from the West of daily minor earthquakes like new smoke from Vesuvius. Jackson was born in Greenville, not long after men reinvented their clocks and thus history, leaving only memory to serve as time's gravity: when men learned to rewrite their history according not to the god that served their own power but rather the idea that served their own power, the age of religion ended and the age of ideology began. The intellectual and memorial corruption of truth took on a new efficiency, ruthlessness a new modern sheen. We have relinquished the definition of American politics to the false faith of the American Right, which so obsequiously professes to love its country even as it holds in contempt the truest and most difficult things for which the country stands; and the bad faith of the American Left, which has been too guilty too long of precisely what it's been accused, hating its country. In the midst of hypocrisy and hate have died guilt and innocence as matters of spiritual or conscionable resolution; rather they've become factors of power as held by ideology. The moral bankruptcy of the American Left as manifested in the Sixties' contention that one is part of the problem if he's not part of the solution—as, of course, the solution is defined by the American Left—lies in the way the individual conscience is taken hostage by orthodoxy, the way it justifies how innocents may be targeted not despite the fact they're innocent, as in war, but rather because they're innocent, which is the basic tactical tenet of terrorism. Jackson was born in Greenville where the Crescent stops before dawn: three hours this side of Atlanta. Born of slave America, outlaw America, mad America, a panic of race and legacy, Negrorighteous and Irish honkycursed and Amerindianravaged, the black genes of him stalking the white, the bastard of him stalking the proud, the guilty of him stalking the innocent. Within his eyes as within the eyes of the land the two guises of the truth have to turn to face each other; it's not likely either can utterly stand what it sees. It's in the aftermath of the mutually appalled vision that there are left the lonely hearts, the cheated, Jackson's own dispossessed and despised and damned as he's called them, who hunt the presence of the American river where nothing's so large it can't be destroyed and nothing's so small it can't be saved.

The protestations of both Left and Right about Jackson's blackness, the first arguing that only his blackness has prevented him from going farther, the second that only his blackness has allowed him to go this far, are the kind of ideological manifestations of what none of us understands about the race of America, and the consequences of its two original sins: what it did to the Indians who belonged here, what it did to the Africans who did not. They pretend Jackson can be removed from his blackness, either to benefit or detriment, and that the meaning of him can be removed from the meaning of his blackness as well. This in turn would remove Jackson from the questions of faith, good bad true and false, which he has raised as profoundly as did Ronald Reagan in his way, or perhaps more profoundly, because Reagan raised the question of faith for those who'd once had it and lost it, while Jackson raises it for those who never had it at all and would once have jeered anyone who told them they had a right to it. They do not jeer Jackson. Only Jackson makes them accept the idea that George Wallace may be redeemed, that a former Ku Klux Klan member in Texas can change to the point of supporting a black preacher for the presidency. Jackson gives his radicalism a common humanity, as Reagan gave his conservatism; Jackson has severed the Left from the cold brutal proposition that the Iowa farmer who is not part of their solution is part of the problem: Jackson acknowledges the farmer has his own problems, as harsh and desperate in their fashion as the problems of Harlem or Watts or South Chicago. Jackson then has proposed to give not only Americans on the Left their faith, but also Americans on the Right their individual innocence. He's left to speak to matters for which he and only he seems to have a special moral authority; and from this he came, for instance, to co-opt an issue thought to be the possession of the American Right, drugs. And while drugs has been a phony issue to the extent that it implies grand political solutions to dilemmas of the spirit, it doesn't change the fact that Jackson speaking on drugs has made Nancy Reagan speaking on drugs a comparatively hollow experience indeed. Jackson can hold his fingers high and show the dirt beneath his nails. From this place of moral authority other amazements follow more naturally: the embrace of white Iowa farmers, the acclamation of bluecollar white unionists in Illinois, the stirred exhilarated disbelief of white kids in Wisconsin. Jackson uses them all for his own political ends but they use him as well, and in the using the believer in Jackson stalks the opportunist. In the process he may yet teach people to love their country even as they hold to their bitterest criticisms of it. He may, in the tradition of all great American political con men, grow into his con and be transformed by it, and come to acknowledge that whatever motivated its original biases and devices has not obstructed the force of truth in it: this happened to Franklin Roosevelt and Robert Kennedy and Ronald Reagan, three keenly brilliant opportunists who nonetheless became seized themselves by opportunity, and by the hopes of other people which became attached to that opportunity. So the dialectic of what people feel about Jesse Jackson swings on, to that time when even as the matter of Jackson's blackness recedes, so will recede the ridiculous hypotheticals of what-if-Jesse-weren't-black. We will deal with his blackness because in all our hearts we find it impossible to believe black people can ever really forgive America for what it did to them, and therefore we wonder how blacks could ever love America at all. As it happens, blacks may yet come to love America most of all. As it happens, they of all people may come to pass through the tunnel of America, darkest pit of it to brightest light of its end, with some truth of it none of the rest of us will know. And it's Jesse Jackson's genius not simply that he knows how to say this but that he says it so often and passionately that he's also come to believe it.

Three hours north of Atlanta, and one hour east of dawn. I ride into the South feet first. I'm on the upper bunk; she sits beneath me, watching out the window into the Carolina night. My compartment is on the side of the train away from the dawn; she'll be the last to see the light, then, except for me, who'll see it after her. "It's only faith that ever believes," I say to her, "that we'll see it at all." We haven't spoken in a while. She's been waiting to tell me. I'm almost asleep when she finally begins to speak, and I wake to her with a start. *When he was a young man* Sally begins to speak *in the Virginia legislature before the Revolution the law was that no man could free his own slaves. An owner had to persuade the state to let him free his own slaves, in this way the owners were as bound to us by the law as we to them. Thomas inherited slaves from his family and many more from his*

*wife's family. In the legislature he wrote a law that would allow
an owner in Virginia to free his own slaves. The law did not pass.
Over the years that came before and after the Revolution he wrote
laws that would loosen the bonds of slave to owner and owner to
slave: none passed.* I feel an inexplicable pang when she says this,
and then I sense it's her pang, when she continues *The truth is
that if the slaves had been freed in those years after the Revolution
I would never have been his lover. I know this. It was in the nature
of the times and in the nature of America that a woman like me
could only have been loved by a white man if I was owned by him.
I know this is so. I was the daughter of my mother by Thomas' own
father-in-law, which is to say that Thomas' wife was my halfsister,
though nearly a generation divided us in age. Thomas' wife may
or may not have known this, she did not confess it if she did. Later
after the Revolution, when Thomas might have freed the slaves he
did not, even as he was obsessed with the idea of it. Because the
truth is Thomas loved the things he owned and would not give
them up, thus I've come to see his obession with the freedom of the
slaves was his obsession with his own ownership. I've come to see
how he tried to force the nation he invented to force him in turn
to accept the things he believed. He wanted the nation to imprison
him with his goodness, because all the goodness of him went into
the invention of America and what was left was the darkness that
owned me first and took my body for its pleasure later. At no time
in his nights did he ever fear God or Judgment Day so much as he
did in the pit of his dark ownership. He never pretended it was
right. I'm less certain of my own pretenses. It felt right and
delirious when he came to me, the semen of the saint coursing
through me.*

*In Paris I was a free woman when I brought his daughter to
him, even at fourteen I was free. His ownership did not cross the
Atlantic with me. He knew this, I knew this. I had a choice. When
he returned to America I did not have to return with him. What
would I have become in Paris, the creole courtesan, quadroon*

queen of a Frenchman? Perhaps I would have led my own revolution, perhaps something of me lay waiting to be created that night I lay in Thomas' bed and we heard them haul down the prison walls in the Paris streets. I had this choice. For a while I thought about why I made the choice I made, I've stopped thinking about it since. I don't know where in my body, at what point near my heart, the arteries of me became those of love; I might suspect I never loved him at all. But I chose to go with him and he changed then. From then until he died he spoke for emancipation but never fought for it, as he had as a young man: when he loved me he had to choose to love his invention of America less, and settle for a more sullied notion of what that invention meant to be. She stops for a bit, having said this; she stops abruptly enough I might think she's not there anymore, except for the new fraught thickness of her last words, which tells me she's still there but the courage to go on is perhaps not. *He was only a man* she says. She doesn't quite believe it. *When he became president he was the most loved man in America that ever lived except the General, he was the most hated too. He had more than any man who had come before or would come again for half a century the presence and authority and power to free the slaves. He did not take this opportunity. I won't say why* and she has to stop again. *I know why* she whispers bitterly. I barely hear her over the clatter of the train. *I know. I know he could not have kept me. In freeing America he would have freed himself to the goodness he'd meant for America, he of all men could not have kept his slaves and without slavery he could not have kept me. Not a colored woman living in his bedroom. It was only slavery that made the way we loved and coupled possible. Thus* and there's a funny sound, like something in the pipes of the train, and in the heat of Leap Summer I think the last water in the pipes of the train has rebelled and is escaping us, but it's the water of her misery and guilt, she sobs onto Atlanta, the tinge of dawnblue in the window now *thus when I chose to go back to America with him as his slave I chose for all slaves in America. I gave him his darkness and allowed him to corrupt his vision: I changed America, I mean. I went back with him, his obsession for emancipation disintegrated into words without fire, he forsook the chance to change America as president and thus doomed America to its inclination to betray itself. Thus for fifty years the poison of the way they owned us, and thus the vicious surgery by which America exhumed its poison blood, its white children dressed in blue killing its white children dressed in gray for the sake of its black children dressed in white. All of it reduced to a choice I made as a fourteen-year-old girl in Paris on a single night in the smoke of the Bastille coming through the window above our love.*

"Go to sleep," I can only finally say, when she says nothing else, and she says *Yes I'll sleep now.* Now then I near Atlanta feet first, the hub of America's doom, where Jesse Jackson as descendant of the choice Sally Hemings made will aspire to the position of state her lover held one hundred seventy-nine years ago. Each time she sees him she must gaze on how that choice marked America, how it sprung loose the choices of every American who ever followed her. In this way she has always been not only what America intended for itself but what it became; and though I sense in her sleep that she sees only the guilt, there is also the redemption. No country was ever so born in light and dark, no country has ever been so drawn to the event horizon where the one begins and the other ends. There are no Jesse Jacksons in any other country of the world, none whose con is so heavy with the bargains by which those who make and keep them redeem themselves. She after all made the Jeffersonian choice, she accepted the premise that the state must subvert itself at moments to birthrights unshakable and beyond challenge: the womb of her pursued its happiness right down into the black clock of history. She chose in that pursuit to love and ravish the man who invented the country that promised to free those it imprisoned with the very promise. That America became what it became was due not as much to her lover's darkness as to the fact that he lacked the nerve of his darkness: he might have freed the rest and kept her his secret still, understanding that everyone has his secret America. The secret America of Jesse Jackson still scares the hell out of too many people, and maybe they're right. The secret America of the others who have run for president this year scared no one, save Gary Hart's and Pat Robertson's and perhaps Robert Dole's: that secret conceived in the flash and wild spinning minutehands of the nuclear imagination. No one is ready for such secrets, least of all the one each of us knows only himself: I have mine. In its shadow my conscience concedes to my sanity over and over. In a life of secrets I can barely name let alone face, I say to her, each of us deserves one secret that makes him happy. You remain mine, I say. But she's asleep, and may not have heard me over the sound of the train. The next time I say it she'll hear too well; and go.

I was watching a tape not so long ago. It was a tape of that speech at the convention in San Francisco that Jesse Jackson gave four years ago. I was watching it and several minutes into it, as the camera swung to Jackson's left, it caught a view of the platform behind his podium; it was filled with Jackson's entourage—family and supporters and campaign aides, there on the platform at the front of the Moscone Center. Almost without exception, they were black faces: one, seated six or seven places away from Jackson, in the front row, was not. It was the face of Michael Dukakis. When I saw this I sat straight up, backed up the tape, and looked again, because I didn't believe my own eyes. Not only was it rather incredible, that Dukakis should be sitting up on Jackson's platform with Jackson's supporters in 1984, but it also didn't make a lot of sense: what was he doing there? I don't remember seeing him four years ago, but then I don't remember that four years ago I would have quite known who Dukakis was to see him. Dukakis, of all people. Several times through Jackson's speech the camera shifted to the same view, and there was no question that it was indeed Dukakis. It remained a mystery to me throughout the speech, and throughout the furor that followed the speech, and the gospel song and the clasping of hands that took place throughout the convention hall in the exhilarated aftermath. After that, people left. The convention night was over. I made my way back to my hotel. Now four years later I watched it on tape, and it was some twenty minutes or so after people had left the hall, when Dan Rather sat in the CBS booth above the Moscone Center discussing the events of the evening, which is to say Jackson's evening, first with Bill Moyers and then Walter Cronkite, that there was a view of the booth from the convention floor, Rather and Cronkite seen through the glass of the booth. And there, on the tape, I could see briefly in the reflection of the booth's glass the face of Michael Dukakis. He was reflected in the booth's glass because at this particular moment he was at the podium addressing the convention. This was why he was sitting on the Jackson platform, occasionally listening to Jackson, occasionally just staring out into the convention hall; he was the speaker scheduled to follow Jackson. In memory, there was no speaker after Jackson; in lore, the convention ended that night with the catharsis of Jackson's confession and declaration. In fact, Michael Dukakis addressed the convention next, a convention that did not see him, that had already emptied itself in body and heart out into the streets of San Francisco, a convention that paid him no mind, that recorded not a moment of his presence, during which the cameras found him to be of such little consequence that they sacrificed his speech entirely to the ruminations of Dan Rather and Walter Cronkite; and all that was noted of Michael Dukakis on this night was a three-second reflection in the window of the CBS booth high above the convention floor.

• • •

For some time now I've been a resident of a hotel called the Perimeter North, allegedly in Atlanta. From anyplace in this hotel, Atlanta is nowhere in sight. If one wants to actually be in

Atlanta, he catches a shuttle from the hotel to a station where a train takes him into the city. From the window of my hotel room I can see several convergent highways, and the wasted wilds of Georgia struggling to hold back the brown of the heat that eats its way from tree to tree across the floor of the South. The halls of the hotel sag with sweat, like the skies of a country that will not rain. My hotel is nonetheless full on this infernal weekend of July; journalists and writers like myself have been assigned here by the housing committee of the Democratic Party, though I don't meet a one of these people until my last day here, a guy from Cape Cod radio who has covered the political evolution of Michael Dukakis the last fifteen years. Nor do any of the people I see here in this hotel appear as though they might be journalists or writers; in truth the only guests of any discernible identity at all are the Oscar Meyer contingent, who have parked their Weeny-mobile outside in the hotel lot. The Oscar Meyer people wear Weenybuttons as well, so there's no mistaking them. The lot of them, particularly the girls, are freshly scrubbed outside and in. These people are not representatives of some faction or other of the Democratic Party, are they? It isn't possible the Democrats have stooped this low in their attempt to impersonate Republicans, is it? Atlantic in its sprawl is sometimes compared to Los Angeles, and one travels through pockets of it in the same way one travels through Los Angeles; but the pockets of Los Angeles bleed into each other, whereas Atlanta's pockets are actually broken up by woods and forests. Its dispersion may reflect strategies of survival; let's not forget Atlanta's distinction as the only major American city, in the fashion of other major cities of the world, ever to have been wiped off the map by the United States. The Atlantans are obsessed with this. This catastrophe is part of the folklore, and William T. Sherman remains the prominent and demonic wellspring of Atlanta's modern history. So from Sherman's holocaust they built the city again, a phoenix from the ashes as they like to say, and spread it high and low, a guerrilla city that will never make the mistake of amassing its whole in one place again, like a general who will never put all his troops in one place. The downtown section of Atlanta is one of the most nondescript urban centers I've ever laid eyes on. Midtown Atlanta is livelier and even lovely, old and shambling and lush.

Five hours from now the first session of the 1988 Democratic Convention begins. One hour ago, in the Hyatt Regency downtown, its final resolution was reached as Dukakis, Jesse Jackson and Lloyd Bentsen, the senator from Texas, held a press conference. Nothing and everything was revealed, and given the events and rhetoric of the last week, which have been testy to say the least, and the mood of things last night at a party held by the California delegation up in Atlanta's high-rent area, Buckhead, and the vertiginous swirl of rumor and conjecture, never has so little said been so remarkable in the course of this campaign, or has such an image of these three men standing together seemed so unlikely. The California party itself was loud and awful and congested, but it's part of the spectacle of these affairs; and having missed the infamous fete thrown four years ago in San Francisco by Willie Brown, the speaker of the California Assembly, it seemed important I investigate. I hit the Greek Democrats' shindig first in the Hyatt, which is the home base of the Dukakis campaign, and linked by skywalks to the Marriott, the home base of the Jackson campaign; my press credential got me in with a warm welcome and a request that I *not* interview any of the delegates. What a sacrifice! I have to eat their food and drink their liquor and not talk to any of them! This was after a weekend of running around from one "newsbreaking" event to the next, always missing whatever news had just broken: if there was a riot in the small parking lot outside the convention center which the Democrats cordoned off for whatever pitiful resistance movement wants to take advantage of it for the moment, I could count on being there fifteen minutes after it happened. The big news on

Sunday was what didn't happen: the press conference called by Dukakis' campaign manager, Susan Estrich, at which after some thirty minutes it became clear Estrich wasn't going to show and instead we were going to hear any number of Dukakis secondaries search for variations on ways to explain to us what wasn't going to happen and why Estrich wasn't going to be there herself to explain why what wasn't happening wasn't happening. One didn't really need an explanation. The evident fact was that after forty-eight hours of meetings with the Jackson people, the Dukakis people were not crossing any impasses, particularly the one created by Dukakis' announcement five days before that he would offer to the convention the name of Bentsen as his nominee for vice president.

That Dukakis telephoned Jackson with the news of Bentsen's selection only after Jackson had learned the news from a reporter in an airport lobby may have been insult or hardball positioning or honest mistake. The Dukakis people of record have insisted what happened was a communication foulup; Dukakis people of background, and people who've watched Dukakis a long time, laugh contemptuously at anyone foolish enough to believe this. For the three weeks preceding this convention, following a process in which Dukakis assured himself the nomination with more certainty than anyone would have predicted four months ago, Jesse Jackson has been either true to himself and the faith of his followers or, depending on your point of view, a pain in the ass. His decision to continue running for the presidential nomination even after the numbers lined up against him is not only reasonable but, given what his campaign has come to mean for so many people, necessary. At the same time he's been running for the vice presidency in a fashion calculated to leave Dukakis as little maneuvering room as possible, pressing on Dukakis a decision he didn't want to make, and a decision moreover which probably would have served no one well, particularly Jackson, who in terms of temperament and talent is perhaps less cut out to be vice president than anyone alive. For all of Jackson's moving language about how far it would mean he has come to become vice president, he remains one of the few people whom the job is beneath. Jackson has disregarded this in order to raise beyond realistic bounds the hopes and expectations of his followers, belittle Dukakis politically by stripping his campaign and victory of meaning beyond the triumph of organization and efficiency and doggedness, which seem to be the only things Jackson will concede to that triumph, and belittle Dukakis personally as a candidate from whom Jackson can't steal any thunder because, in Jackson's words, Dukakis is bringing to Atlanta no thunder to steal.

The choice of Bentsen, to be sure, is hardly uplifting. He's a Texas moneyman of the old school of politics, the kind of politico against whom Dukakis railed in his purer reform days; and the differences on basic issues between Dukakis and Bentsen are a perfectly legitimate target of Republican scorn, and one that should and will receive relentless attention. In short there's no good reason on earth for Dukakis to get away scotfree with the choice of Bentsen, and even its political efficacy is suspect. Nonetheless the parade of Jackson supporters across the television screens day and night following the selection of Bentsen seems disingenuous if not outright deluded, if we may assume such longtime black Democratic pols as Charles Rangel and Maxine Waters ought to know better. There's much wrath to the effect that Jackson earned the vice presidency and that its being denied to him is explicitly corrupt and implicitly racist. Dukakis on the other hand got the most votes, and in a democracy we call this person the winner and the other one the loser. One senses that over the last few weeks Jackson finally got on Dukakis' nerves, and the governor sensed he was running the risk of having all his buttons pushed by Jackson in public. Jackson keeps talking about a partnership, in terms which he seems to dictate: Dukakis has presumably wondered to himself, What's all this partnership crap? I'm sure, last time I checked, that I won. I ran a long hard campaign, weathered the crises with steadiness, even when Jackson kicked my butt in the Michigan caucus I kept the campaign on a high plane, I kept it on a high plane in New York, I never got nasty, maybe I did this because I'm just an exemplary human being or maybe I did it because I knew the day was coming when I'd have to deal with Jackson and I didn't want any festering wounds of the past to get in the way. Who's inflicting wounds now? Thus the Dukakis irritation. Jackson has been acting like a limelight junkie withdrawing from his addiction in public when the juice of the limelight runs dry. Truly for both him and his supporters what's involved here is not simply the denial of the vice presidency but the denials of three hundred fifty years; Dukakis, however, does not bear the burden of all those denials, not in a fight he won fair, square and clean. Remarkably for someone as liberal as the Republicans would have us believe Dukakis is, he doesn't appear beset by liberal guilt; and he hasn't reacted like the unregenerate racist that Jackson people were calling him in whispers at the California party last night in Buckhead. What allowances Dukakis may have made to Jackson before this morning's news conference are not so much to the race of Jackson's campaign as to the history of it; and if Dukakis has been able to make such a distinction in his own mind, whether consciously or unconsciously, then it demonstrates perhaps more imagination than others have credited to him. Interestingly, the reports filtering out of the meeting describe a scene of two men getting their metaphors straight—Jackson's in which he's likened Dukakis to a plantation owner who accepts the labor of his slaves as something owned by him, Dukakis' likening himself to the team quarterback, in a sport where blacks don't often get to be the quarterback—only to be resolved by, of all people, Lloyd Bentsen, who speaks in accents and nuances more compatible with Jesse than Mike, and who points out that if the Democrats can't get their act together and quickly, their

common need of each other will give way to common blame. If
Dukakis and Jackson actually needed Bentsen to point this out to
them, neither one may be that smart after all.

It may be that this morning ends a rather bad phase of the
Dukakis campaign, one marred not only by the conflicts with
Jackson and attacks by George Bush, but by a couple of other
events that could not bode well. One is a fierce debate among
partisans and commentators as to whether we should be sorry for
blowing up an Iranian airplane, with the current argument
tipping heavily on the side of the unrepentant. This feeling is
rooted most obviously in sentiment about Iran in general, and
perhaps more profoundly in a moral thesis that's genetically
American, which posits that if one means no harm, then no
harm has actually been done for which any apology is necessary
or even appropriate. Intent dictates malice, and only malice truly
dictates evil: this is an extension of Americans' self-image as a
basically unmalicious people. Now the American capacity for
saying sorry has never been so small, and it's pointed out that the
Iranian government never said it was sorry for holding Americans
hostage nine years ago, which is neither here nor there for the
two hundred ninety-odd human beings blown out of the skies as
the result of an American error. It's also not been pointed out in
rebuttal, at least not persuasively, that we're not Iranians, that in
fact there are any number of things we'd like to think we do
differently from Iranians. Thus the best that a significant number
of dead Iranians can hope for is the more formal and passionless
concession of "regret." In our stubborn determination to insist on
ways in which the episode is different from the Soviet shooting of
a Korean airplane some years ago, and of course there are ways
in which the episodes are different, we seem equally determined
to act more like Russians than ever. As the United States has won
the economic and ideological war with the Soviet Union, the
Soviets have won a war of the spirit, compelling us to define
ourselves in the same terms of arrogant ruthlessness. This can't

be good for Dukakis, though he may have enough coldblooded-
ness himself to accommodate it. The second blow to the
Democrats over the last several weeks came from a man named
Meese, who in a relatively short and breathtaking term as
attorney general of the United States has established himself as
one of the most disgraceful public servants in memory. Hostile to
the Bill of Rights, contemptuous of the principle of presumed
innocence for the accused (until he himself became the accused,
at which point he rediscovered the principle), disastrously incom-
petent in the workings of his office, willfully ignorant of the
history of the judicial system in general and the court system in
particular, specifically the Supreme Court, ravenous in his
influence-mongering on behalf of various pals and cronies,
surreptitiously careless in matters of his own finances and taxes,
offensive in his judgments relating to both ethics and politics, he
has lately struck the cruellest blow of all: he quit. Given a joke of
Orwellian proportions, that such a person could actually be the
head of a department named Justice, now the Democrats have
been denied the punchline of Meese's continuous and relentlessly
disastrous presence. So it also seems significant that, this morning, as Dukakis and Jackson and Bentsen were emerging together
from the last few weeks of their discord, there came as well the
announcement of an accepted ceasefire in the Iran-Iraq war, and
the release of a special prosecutor's report on the attorney general
the upshot of which is: we can't indict him but we know he's a
bastard anyway. The ceasefire helps Dukakis in that, if it comes
to pass, it removes still another area of possible international
tension from the campaign, good news indeed for a candidate
who is utterly bereft of any experience in international affairs.
The special prosecutor's report of course will codify some things
Dukakis has to say about the Reagan era in general. I don't
suppose, however, he'll drive home the point too hard, since it
would only alienate the country, because the era has been wholly
true to its own ethos, and those who have navigated the era have

been true to the ethos as well, which says Look Out For Number One and Get Whatever You Can Get Whatever Way It Takes. That the president who gave this ethos such artificial eloquence has been sabotaged by men who lived out these "principles" by peddling influence and corrupting their offices and authoring million-dollar books badmouthing the president is an irony that I personally don't have the magnanimity to regret.

The axiom that "good" conventions, in the sense that they're exciting, make for defeat, and "bad" conventions, in the sense that their conclusions are foregone, make for victory, has proven true in every election since 1964. In the age of television, however, there would seem to be a point at which the convention, becoming dull beyond belief, must necessarily lose its audience, and this would seem particularly true as the conventions become more utterly television events. The paradox is that television, even as it completely defines the political convention, keeps pushing the point further away; the duller the convention gets, the less attention television gives it, which in turn means the convention gets even more packaged and television-tidy, which is to say duller still. We call this a vicious circle. This year, for instance, when the conventions of both parties were doomed to a stultifying dullness after some fairly reasonable speculation early on that one or both might be quite dramatic, the networks reduced their coverage to a mere couple of primetime hours. With this morning's press conference between Dukakis, Jackson and Bentsen, even the most modest prospect of excitement has been diminished; this in contrast to the 1984 San Francisco affair in the hull of the great gray Battleship Moscone, where the Democrats were positively giddy with disaster. The selection of Geraldine Ferraro that year as Mondale's running mate didn't lower the voltage, clearly; her very name rocked the hall with cheers every time it was mentioned at the podium, and one of my most poignant memories is of standing in the men's room and hearing whoever was speaking to the convention at the moment mention for the umpteenth time the next vice president of the United States, Geraldine Ferraro, and as her name floated in through the door the guy next to me muttered a small, happy "Yay" into the yellow puddle of his urinal. Only Jackson's name elicits any similar response in Atlanta. The enthusiasm for Dukakis is no less forced than was the enthusiasm for Mondale; indeed Mondale's may have been warmer, if less pregnant with the respect that attends potential victory.

The Omni Center, where the convention is taking place, is so alarmingly small that it has an adjunct, the far more colossal World Congress Center next door, from which the convention is actually being covered. In truth it is the Omni which is adjunct to the WCC, and operates essentially as a studio, a somewhat impressive light- and soundstage on which the program is produced even as its reality is constructed by the press in the other room. Tonight, when I go to the convention's first session, the congestion is on the order of a rock-concert riot except that there isn't the energy of a rock concert; and the security, which begins stringently enough, will become much more so as the week progresses, far more than at the Moscone four years ago, when I suppose they cared rather less whether anything actually happened to the candidate. People may be crushed to death tonight but no one is going to be trampled underfoot, since no one's ever going to move that fast or excitedly, except for Al Gore. I'm surprised Gore is even here, I thought some gene of humiliation might have discouraged him as it would have deterred anyone with enough sense of self, not only after having been devastated in the New York primary, but also following the vice-presidential boomlet he desperately launched the week after John Glenn's fell to earth and the week before Bentsen's made it into orbit. This development had placed me in a bit of a moral dilemma, and I still hadn't resolved it, when events resolved it for me: in my head I composed one anonymous telegram after another to Michael Dukakis trying to tip him off as to why Gore might just be a distinctly chancy choice. Now, given the logistics at the Omni, not only is Gore tonight frantic to get down onto the convention floor in time for all the introductions being given the year's various losers, but the odds of my bumping into him while he's in this frenzy are perilously realistic. I've already slammed into Paul Simon, whose fame has fled so quickly he must once again be introduced as a senator from Illinois and not a Grammy winner. A reporter next to me, as I'm sitting up in the gallery seats watching Garrison Keillor and Ed Begley, Jr., and Ally Sheedy read cute letters from kids, tells me about having just overheard a security guard say, "I don't care who that man is, he's not getting in without a pass." The reporter adds, "And you know who it was? Al Gore!" I know I'm going to run into Gore, or he's going to see me across a hallway, and his eyes are going to narrow and he's going to remember New York and put two and two together, even though I didn't actually ever send that telegram jettisoning his vice presidency. So I'm sentenced to the galleries listening to Keillor and Begley and Sheedy since I don't dare wander out into the halls. The networks aren't actually broadcasting much of the kids' letters, saving the Democrats once again.

Whether they've also edited the ravings of Paul Kirk, I don't know. Kirk is a Ted Kennedy flunky from Massachusetts who got himself named some years ago as chairman of the Democratic Party, succeeding another egomaniac named Charles Manatt from California. Both Kirk and Manatt are under the impression that being chairman of the Democratic Party is quite a big deal; it may be they remember the days when George Bush was chairman of the Republican Party, forgetting at the same time that Bush was given this job by Richard Nixon because he was so clearly worthless in any position of real importance. Jesse Jackson is not happy with Kirk. He believes, with some justification, that Kirk has played favorites in the case of Dukakis, and he would like Kirk out. Dukakis, from twin standpoints of both loyalty and control, won't remove him, though he may well name Jackson's man Ron Brown, or some other Jackson figure, vice chairman, and part of this morning's deal almost surely includes a lot of Jackson people being moved into the high levels of the party apparatus. Kirk would do the party a favor by giving the job up, but this is after all the man who's managed to get his name plastered on every square inch of the convention, every empty wall or sheet of literature or souvenir or piece of paraphernalia; the only thing that doesn't have "Paul Kirk, Chairman" inscribed on it is the Omni dome itself. Tonight Kirk will get so carried away with himself he nearly talks Jimmy Carter out of prime-time. Carter's rehabilitation is one of the phenomena of the convention, a result of passing time, a second Reagan term that smells worse with every passing moment, and the collapse of integrity for which the Reagan presidency looms like a Colossus of Rhodes straddling the American river. One of the mysteries of American politics is how a man as intelligent and idealistic as Carter could ever have been so unsuccessful as president. Carter has bided his time until the party might answer the mystery in its own way, which is: he wasn't that bad. Carter himself offers his own answer this evening, which is: I wasn't that bad, but I still can't give a decent speech to save my life. The only particularly good speech he ever gave was at the Democratic Convention that nominated him for the first time in 1976, when he was the only president or president-to-be who ever quoted Bob Dylan and did it in a way that suggested he understood the quote and it meant something to him. For a lot of us in 1976 this was no small thing. His speech tonight is awful. His clear failure in communicating with people, wherein lay his failure in leading them, seems resounding; even for Jimmy Carter it's quite a bad speech. It follows the keynote address of Ann Richards, a Texas politician who like other classic Texas politicians including Lyndon Johnson and Jim Wright—but not Lloyd Bentsen—gets folksy to the point of artificiality. Her best moments are a couple when she lights into the Republicans and the pending end of the Reagan-Meese-Deaver-Nofziger-Poindexter-North-Weinberger-Watt-Gorsuch-Lavelle-Stockman-Haig-Bork-Noriega-Bush era; her worst are the ones extolling the virtues and sentiments of the Democratic Party. At any rate Richards' keynote does not seem destined for political legend as was Barbara Jordan's in 1976 or Mario Cuomo's in 1984, when both ignited serious talk of drafts for the vice presidency and presidency respectively.

The fire of the convention then, and its memory, is left once again to Jesse. It will come Tuesday night, in a platform fight that has been curtailed as part of the bargain struck Monday morning, and in Jackson's speech. There's talk Tuesday morning that Jackson is something of a broken man, bitterly dispirited by the way things have gone down; but given the messianic nature of Jackson's campaign, it may be that it couldn't have transpired any other way. Dukakis' greatest failure is in not understanding that messianic leadership begets messianic followership, which is to say Jackson is yoked to his followers in a way leaders whose following is less passionate, which is to say someone like Michael Dukakis, are not. Maybe Jackson didn't understand this either, or didn't until he was in very deep. While we may say what we want about Jackson's ego, and while there have been many occasions in the last few weeks when it appeared to be veering seriously out of control, putting Dukakis in a position where he had to take control, it's also true that Jackson has been a man under the pressure of expectations which lesser leaders never feel, short of being president. This may constitute Jackson's greatest experience to be president. That Jackson has raised these expectations himself is incontrovertible; so is it incontrovertible that America, rather than the United States, raises such expectations. It's part of the function of America as idea. In retrospect, a dinner which took place on the Fourth of July between the Jacksons and the Dukakises at the Dukakis home appears more disastrous than the missed phone call by which Dukakis failed to inform Jackson about the choice of Bentsen for vice president. It was not unreasonable that Jackson went to the dinner expecting to have a serious discussion with Dukakis about, among other things, the vice presidency; this never came about and left Jackson stranded in terms of developing a tack for dealing with his messianic supporters and preparing them for the inevitable realities. He felt he had no alternative but to turn up the heat on Dukakis during the days that followed. Dukakis may not bear the burden of history's denials to blacks but he does bear the burden of understanding what those denials have meant, and his own political life will be easier when he understands that what Jackson means to his supporters is not necessarily the same as whatever relationship Dukakis may feel he has with his own. Both Dukakis and Jackson have things to sort out here this week. The ice just about can't get thinner beneath either one; they're barely on the same lake as it is. Signs have already appeared outside the Omni: "Jesse, kick Mike's ass, don't lick it." This may be just fringe stuff. A meeting with Jackson and many of his delegates at the Marriott Marquis Monday afternoon goes well; even Maxine Waters is placated to some extent.

When I walk out onto the floor of the convention on Tuesday, I don't sense much electricity or tension; everything feels particularly and intently oiled; the only thing that creaks is the actual floor itself. I stand next to a large man who leads the California delegation when it's time to applaud and who coaxes them on their votes, depending on what the leadership has worked out regarding the platform and the two of a dozen minority planks on which Dukakis would not make concessions. The large man is inescapably like the guy who churns up the audience at the taping of a TV game show, and nothing's been left to chance; it's been prearranged by both the Dukakis and Jackson forces what's to be won and what's to be lost. The Jackson people, particularly the black delegates, don't like Dukakis much and won't even talk about Bentsen, but already details are leaking out about what Jackson's gotten in the bargain, including a vice chairmanship of the party for one of his own, and some fifteen other seats on the national committee. In terms of future campaigns this is not insignificant. The only crisis that rises is some five hours later: the Primetime Crisis, which is an extension of the Primetime Reality that has come to dictate Democratic Conventions ever since that surreal night in 1972 when George McGovern accepted the nomination of the party at two in the morning. Jackson's scheduled to speak before ten-thirty, at the peak of television primetime. When he's not on at ten-forty, many of the Jackson people are about to have fits. The Omni is filled to the gills; the doors have been shut by fire marshals, actually locking outside a number of delegates and luminaries, including Ann Richards, as well as media and guests. I've been in my seat four hours and don't much understand or sympathize with anyone foolish enough to arrive late or to step outside the hall for a moment before the speech, as some have done. This is the extent to which Jackson has dominated the convention; and for the Democrats to fuck up now on the matter of when he gets on TV strikes me as an inconceivable bungle. As it happens, the party has canceled quite a few major speakers in a frantic attempt to get on schedule, but the black woman next to me isn't going to be impressed by that: "They're not going to let him on national TV," she mutters bitterly. The tension of which this convention's been emptied all day comes back into the hall. There is of course the irony that Jesse Jackson, who is notoriously late for almost every function or event on his behalf, including the television special that ran on the eve of the California primary for which hundreds of thousands of dollars were spent to broadcast fifteen minutes of an empty chair, should now be late for his greatest moment, or should for once be on time only to find it's everyone else who's late. The delay, moreover, is prolonged by Jackson's own introduction, a nice one by his kids, and a very effective little film set to Jackson Browne's "For America" and Ray

Charles' "America the Beautiful," two musical selections which say a lot about the tone and intent of Jackson's 1988 campaign. Jackson begins to speak at eleven.

It doesn't even take a moment of suspended disbelief to imagine it is Jackson accepting the nomination of the party. The party could not receive him with more emotion; he stands on the platform embraced by the party bosses; he's fought his way to the inner circle of the party; what's happening in the convention hall now, the spectacular explosion of red Jackson signs giving way to the dark as he speaks, which in turn is splattered with the ellipses of light from the cameras, may well be the beginning of another phase that will win him the nomination outright four or eight years from now, though one also understands that Jackson's arc may have been drawn as far as it will ever go. It occurs to me at this moment that this is in fact the end. That something has peaked here and must give way to something else—though it seems too that Jackson's followers, as did Reagan's, can only continue to insist on his irresistibility, following him until he's fulfilled or dead. In my own particular generation of American politics, Jackson's connection with this many people on a level this primal has been matched only by Ronald Reagan and Robert Kennedy; it doesn't seem anything about the evening can be matched in heart or spirit two nights from now when Dukakis speaks. There's still much growing up to do among Jackson's followers: the ideologues of the Left adore him as thoughtlessly as the ideologues of the Right have adored Reagan, which is always at least embarrassing and at most frightening; and if the black delegates may be forgiven a similar adoration, given the dearth of hope American politics has imposed on them so long and the bounty of hope to which Jackson speaks in contrast, there's still the lack of recognition on their part that for many honest people Jackson is unacceptable not because of race but because his politics sound radical beyond realism or reason, and his messianic appeal appears to make him a naive, even fantastic prospect for president. It may be for these reasons Jackson's come to see his future in neither the ideologues nor even necessarily the blacks, but in dispossessed whites of largely conservative instincts: he speaks to them tonight when he reminds his audience that most of America's poor are not black or brown but are young white women with children and without husbands. Progressives and conservatives must find the common ground, he tells the convention tonight: hawks and doves are birds of a feather. This is startlingly new coming from Jesse Jackson. He hasn't diluted his convictions by expanding his perspective: his implicit vision is not that America is a bad place, as the Left would have had it even five years ago, but that it's a good place that can be made even better. He may understand that in no other Western country, including those that condemned the United States for slavery a hundred and fifty years ago, could Jesse Jackson have come this far: "America is better than that," he will say with an insistent sorrow as he recounts its injustices. It's sorrow that's replaced rage. In Jackson's rhetoric, then, America lives and not simply the United States. And if it's a statement of Jackson's ego that his own concerns and those of the people he leads have become intermingled in his own mind to the point of never being separated again, it's also part of this vision that his own past is an accurate metaphor for something much bigger, and that his childhood informs his concerns, that the vision of triumph is informed by his failures. Leading the resurrection, for instance, he's come to see Jimmy Carter as a tragic figure, another man of largely conservative instincts who nonetheless had his ideals, but more than that a figure whom destiny betrayed, and a reminder to Jackson that destiny isn't always just, nor is it without its chaos. Jackson can speak to his own past as Dukakis can't, or at least can't with the same convincing passion; with Dukakis, allusions to the past are always concessions to public relations. Jackson speaks to his past this evening and maybe it's the cynical pitch of the shaman; but if you believe him, and we all believe the con

man we want to believe, then you call it empathy. "Jesse
Jackson," he says, and now Jackson comes to the end of his
speech, now he's completely taken flight from the original text,
now he speaks to himself in the way the dispossessed may be
speaking to him as well at this moment, "Jesse Jackson, you don't
understand my situation. You be on television, you don't
understand. I see you with the big people, you don't understand
my situation." And then, "I understand. You're seeing me on
TV but you don't know the real me that makes me me. They
wonder why does Jesse run, because they see me running for the
White House, they don't see the house I'm running from," and
this is an entirely different sort of confession from that of his 1984
speech: this is a confession of triumph that's been informed by
failure. In the hall this is the risk of lost control that, sooner or
later, is taken by all great artists. "I have a story," he says in a
sweat, "I wasn't always on television. Writers were not always
outside my door. When I was born late one afternoon, October
Eighth in Greenville South Carolina, no writers asked my
mother her name. Nobody chose to write down our address. My
mama was not supposed to make it. I was not supposed to make
it. . . . I understand. I know abandonment. People being mean
to you, saying you're nothin' nobody, can never be anything. I
understand. Jesse Jackson's my third name. I'm adopted. When
I had no name my grandmother gave me her name, my name
was Jesse Burns until I was twelve. So I wouldn't have a blank
space, she gave me a name to hold me over. I understand when
nobody knows your name. I understand when you have no
name. I understand. . . . Every one of those funny labels they
put on you, those of you watching this broadcast tonight in the
projects, on the corners, I understand. Call you outcast, low-
down, you can't make it. You're nothing, you're from nobody,
subclass underclass. . . . When you see Jesse Jackson, when my
name goes in nomination, *your* name goes in nomination. I was
born in the slum but the slum was not born in me. And it wasn't

born in you, and you can make it, wherever you are tonight you can make it. Hold your head high . . . you can make it. It gets dark sometimes but the morning comes, don't you surrender. Suffering breeds character, character breeds faith: and in the end, faith will not disappoint." The audience is lost to him now and he is lost to them. "America will get better and better." I haven't the slightest idea whether Jesse Jackson would ever actually be a good president. But where he goes, by whatever alchemy of what he shows combined with what we see, the land beneath him is more American than the land beneath either Dukakis or George Bush; and in that space is promised a hundred more visions, some at the abyss, some in the distance and speed with which the dream of Jackson has been to flee the abyss.

Sally. Come away from the abyss then. You've been at the edge long enough to have the appearance of one hoping to fall over; you don't deserve that. You've lived too many years in the pit of your guilt, it isn't right you've taken this burden alone, the burden of having said Yes when in Paris Jefferson said to you, Come home with me as my slave. Even Jefferson the best of us was marked by the dark glee of what he loved to own; that Americans loved to own each other is not your sin. I have here in my hand the earring you lost the first night I met you. *Yes, he gave it to me in Paris when I said I would go with him. He did not mean it that way but I still thought to myself then, This is his gift to me for the choice I've made, small price. A pair of earrings, small price.* Sally: once I said the wrong thing too. Once I wrote something I shouldn't have; it had consequences I never imagined. I thought like all Americans that malice had to lie at the root of sin, that if one was innocent in his intentions he was innocent in his actions. Someone else paid for this. *And I thought it was a small price for me to pay, if I just took the earring and gouged it into the flesh of my lobe, pierced my own ear with his gift; small price; but I did it just the same. They bled for weeks. They bled, my ears, to America. They bled, my ears, when I looked over the ship's side, small red price dropping onto the bleached foam of the Atlantic.* If you forgive yourself, then I can forgive me too. I don't know if Americans believe too easily in their own redemption, I only know I've never quite believed in mine.

It's twenty-four hours after Jesse Jackson, the third day of the convention; and I've decided not to go to the convention tonight. Tonight the convention will nominate Michael Dukakis, and Jackson by proxy will move to make it unanimous. The artificiality of the last week has blown some cylinder in me at last, if only because last night escaped artificiality in some profound unsettling fashion: nothing of this life, from airconditioned hotel to sweltering wastes of Atlanta's northern perimeter to airconditioned mass-transit train to sweltering downtown Atlanta to airconditioned hotel again, is tolerable much longer. Then the well-documented television reality underscores the futility of anything that feels like a personal experience, which is to say the speech Jackson gave to those of us who were at the convention is not the speech he gave to those watching it on television. I sit in the convention hall, a firsthand witness to the proceedings, and return to the Perimeter North at night to call my friends three thousand miles away in Los Angeles so they can tell me what really happened, because what they saw on television *is* what really happened. I spend tonight in sultry Midtown, characterized by the vibrancy of sinners, part of Atlanta uninterested in the rectitude of history or the pretensions of a Major American City; I have dinner, about nine o'clock wander into a club called the Cheetah, have a seat at the bar, order a couple of drinks, and after twenty minutes or so it comes to my attention that there are about forty perfectly naked women dancing on the tables around me. I strike up a conversation with one who goes by the name of Trixie but whose real name, she confides, is Cricket. She is twenty and was the daughter of a hippie. By my calculations she was conceived around the time I was graduating high school, in the tumultuous year of 1968. Cricket laments that while she would like to go to California the men there wouldn't like her because her hair is black and her skin is white and her body is lush rather than blond and tan and lean. She has the saddest smile I've ever seen. It's sad not simply because it's desperate for joy but because she draws it out of her to offer as a gift to make you happy. Some guy next to her says idiotic things to her about her body, though this is not to preclude that whatever I've said to her isn't idiotic as well in its own way. Cricket can only suffer the fools so long, I think she does well here in this club but not as well as Sheena, the blonde who Cricket explains is her sister, which I know perfectly well is a fiction. All the girls of the Cheetah have fictions, and they're entitled to them given what they reveal. Are most of the men the same? I ask. She nods. What do you think when you dance? I ask. I laugh at the men, she says, they amuse me. After a moment she explains, Only the artists really like me. She has a cat named Alex who was her lover in a past life.

After a while I say goodbye to Cricket and go back to the Perimeter North. The sky is smoky from fireworks, celebrating Dukakis' nomination. At three in the morning my hotel room is vacant of any sign of the world except the flashing red light on my telephone; when the front desk tells me it's a message from my mother, I know something is wrong. I call Astrid. She tells me I should ignore my mother's instructions to call her the next morning and instead call now, when it's midnight in Los Angeles. I sense her intuition is right on this matter. That my mother is awake and answers the phone immediately is confirmation that something extraordinary has happened: my father's had a double bypass today. "I didn't know whether to tell you," my mother says. You should always tell me, I say. "I didn't know if I was ready," she says, meaning she could cry at any moment, "and there was nothing for you to do. You wouldn't have been able to get back in time for the surgery, and there was no point taking you away from your work." Yes, well, I'm thinking contritely, tonight my work was talking to a naked girl in a bar. I call Astrid back and tell her I'll be in L.A. in a couple of days. Throughout the rest of the night, caught to my dreams is the image of my father, tubes running in and out of him like memories through a moment.

• • •

In the summer of 1988 my father in Los Angeles is frail to see. He's sore from the way he's been broken open and repaired, and short of breath; when we talk he gasps for words. The problem began in one leg, the blood passages constricted by fifty years of nicotine; two arteries to the heart were almost completely closed. Dad's sixty-eight. A friend of mine, in the meantime—an editor for a local magazine—collapses one afternoon under the coming barrage of a massive coronary; he is seven years older than I. His third night in intensive care I'm advised by phone he may not make it; some time later he says to me from his hospital bed, "I died twice." Not given to metaphysics, he does not have any recollections of white lights at the edge of life; he did, however, go to a place where he had a choice. He went to a place where he had a choice between dying and living, in which the life of his heart was so painful, and the seduction of painless death so beguiling, that the choice was not only uneasy but braver than one could imagine such a choice being. I suppose there are other hearts across the Southwest that have leapt their extra day, only to find midjump that the other side was farther than they supposed, only to look downward midjump at the chasm below them, how far it drops, how the bottom is actually beyond vision.

In the wake of my return, one of our neighbors has moved and, in the process, our original five cats have multiplied to eleven, the neighbor having left hers behind. Now cats camp on the front porch, they scale our windows. They slither through openings trying to get into the apartment, they squirm through every crevice and cranny. They attach themselves by their claws to the window screens; the world of our little apartment has been transformed to a siege. Isn't this like something I once *made up?* One small one, a nursing mother, is relentless like out of a horror film: chase her, threaten her, attack her, ignore her, she returns anyway; you could drop a bomb on her and the cat from hell will be there an hour later when you open your door. Our original cats must battle their way through the invasion to get inside the house; the cranky asthmatic one climbs the tree in front and leaps from its branches to a two-inch sill where he sits breathing heavily outside our second-floor window. He hits the wall so hard he knocks out the pilot light in the heater downstairs. Sometimes he slips and from inside downstairs we see a furry meteor drop to earth. At last the neighbor comes and takes them, including one of our original five; such a sudden peace falls on the neighborhood as to seem suspicious.

I'm being audited. The news came some months ago, it arrives in a letter you have to sign for. My accountant who deals with matters relating to the vast Erickson fortune is taking care of this. The year for which I'm being audited, 1985, was the one in which I ceased to be a journalist and began to be a novelist, which is to say my income that year was my all-time postadolescent low, $7,875. After deductions the adjusted gross income was $3,687. The Internal Revenue Service has spent several months investigating my very complex business dealings. They have interviewed me as to my life and residence and work, and in regards to all my various accounts and assets, which for the most part comprise in total a 1983 Toyota. They've gotten down to the nitty-gritty of my income and deductions, on all of which I've provided rather detailed information. By now the basics of the case have been established and substantiated but the government still is not satisfied, I have a new round of questions to answer on my return to Los Angeles. Virtually all my friends, agents and editors have explained to me as calmly as possible that of course this is politically instigated, and point to this interview or that which came out after my second book where I said things about the current government which might lead one to believe I have not been an active footsoldier in the Reagan Revolution. My accountant insists a computer is to blame.

In the summer of 1988 Los Angeles is a ghost town since one of the city's major cottage industries is on strike. The strike is conducted by the people who write movies and television, and naturally my sympathies are with them. Obviously it's an outrage that a writer would be asked to settle for a mere $150,000 after producing a whole season's worth of sparkling "Who's the Boss?" episodes. Not to mention the horror stories of financially strapped writers having to sell the horses right off their Malibu ranches. All right, so I don't sound very sympathetic. Still, the writers' willingness to submit the issue to arbitration, and the resistance to this recourse by the producers, speak for themselves. The strike is now in its fifth month. My brother-in-law is a playwright who's in his second year of writing and producing a moderately popular and respected TV drama; having cast his lot with the writers he has been asked by the guild to speak to groups as an example of a writer-producer (hyphenates, they're called in the business) who knows where his conscience lies. To a large extent he has never been sanguine in his soul about writing television and looks to the day he'll return to his art. Thus his choice is, as well as a matter of political conscience, a personal declaration to himself that he remains a writer despite the hyphenation of his recent résumé; he's unnerved by all the people who tell him he's courageous. "They keep telling me how courageous I am," he says over the phone, "what do they know that I don't?" The restaurants and diners and shops and secretarial services in Hollywood that cater to the studios are empty because there's no business; the people I know who work in the business are scared. By later July there's still not an end in sight; when the end does come it's as sudden as the end of the cats, and there's an unspoken feeling of defeat among the writers.

The University of Southern California has called to offer me a job teaching fiction writing. I would replace T. Coraghessan Boyle, who is off somewhere spending his Guggenheim and has suggested my name in his stead. This is what it's come to, then: I've become respectable enough, *safe* enough, to teach children how to write. It's appalling. Surely there must be a mistake; the university hasn't actually read anything I've written, right? Not in a thousand years, I respond to the offer with scornful bravado, but only in my head; what in fact comes out of my mouth is something like, "Gosh, what an honor. I don't know what to say. Not this year, I'm afraid, but thanks very much for asking, and thank Tom for the recommendation, please keep me in mind for some future occasion."

I hear gunshots from my bedroom window. One night a crazy person from MacArthur Park walks right into our apartment on my wife, who has the nerve and presence of mind to chase him right back out; a week later two people are robbed at gunpoint in the street before our building. The gangs of East and South Central Los Angeles spill up into the barrio where we live and even to the edges of Hancock Park. Children on the wrong corners of the wrong nights die for their error. Even in this year the casual randomness is startling and dehumanizing.

As the strike in Hollywood ends, the industry unwittingly and no doubt against all its truest instincts produces the only really dangerous cultural event of the year. It is, of all things, Jesus. In defiance of longlaid publicity plans Universal Pictures advances the release date of an American movie by Martin Scorsese based on a Greek novel by Nikos Kazantzakis; a local critic invites me to a prerelease screening. The picture has unleashed a storm of commentary across the world, almost none of it based on anyone's having actually seen the picture; people who call themselves and may even consider themselves Christians protest the film fervently and threaten one way or another to prevent people from seeing it. It doesn't take twenty minutes before I realize, watching *The Last Temptation of Christ*, that this is indeed a dangerous picture and that those who are afraid of it ought to be afraid. None of this has anything to do with the picture's being anti-Christian or a slander against Jesus; in fact it's a deeply Christian film, with Jesus portrayed more heroically than he has ever been before, at least in the movies. And that's what's dangerous about the film, because the heroism extends from his humanity rather than his divinity, it extends from the way his humanity over the course of his life must struggle to attain the grace and courage of people at their most divine. One particularly earnest and evenhanded radio editorial suggests, after the picture opens, that both sides have won something: Universal a boxoffice bonanza from all the free publicity; and the Christians from the manner in which people will be moved to consider Jesus and what he believed. But of course this is the last thing the Christians protesting this film can tolerate, the idea that people will be moved to *consider* Jesus; these people protesting the movie have already decided the matter of Jesus, and consideration of that matter only threatens their hold on the idea of Jesus. This Jesus in this movie utterly upends the innocuous Jesus of a thousand Sunday-school sermons; and the most subversive thing about it is the way it not only preserves but reinforces all the imagery and iconography of Christianity, to an extent many Christians won't be able to abide. You want the blood of Jesus, you get the blood of Jesus. The crucifixion in the film is not one to render spiritual glory visually or dramatically benign, there's nothing poetic about it: it's ghastly. It's an execution of such mindboggling pain and humiliation that the courage of a man who chose to go to it is incontrovertible; but because the film makes this vivid, the emphasis cannot be escaped: the courage of a *man*. This is the contradiction of Christianity which still thwarts its clear philosophical and mystic logic: the sacrifice of Jesus is meaningless when it's divorced from his humanity. Over two thousand years the Church has struggled to fulfill that divorce; it was not, after all, until several hundred years after Jesus' death that the Church decided he was actually God, rather than the more vague son of God. Thus the Christians trying to suppress the film characterize the film's Jesus, played by Willem Dafoe, as weak, perverted and simple; and thus the critics left to deal with the film are cowed, trying to cut themselves some slack by simply saying it's not a very good movie, even as they take the politically correct position in its constitutional defense. The TV critics offer the most damning judgment of all: it's boring. This is similar to what critics like to say about pornography, as if to trivialize it in such a way there's no point taking a thoughtful position on it. While the picture is open to criticism on a number of levels, you have to be a distinctly stupid individual to find it boring. Boring is the last thing the film is, unless your range of mental stimulation stops somewhere just an inch beyond your eyes. My own guess is that all its flaws notwithstanding, *The Last Temptation* is one of the half dozen really remarkable American films made in this decade; but that's neither here nor there. In the summer of 1988 what's striking is the way the Right seizes on the issue, Robert Dornan of Orange County rising on the floor of the House of Representatives to condemn the picture with every fiber of his being, as I believe he put it (he as well has not seen the movie); and in particular the way the religious politicians use the picture as a vehicle for their notable venom, Jerry Falwell, Donald Wildmon, the anti-Semite minister R. J. Hymers, and a Mother Angelica, her face a mass of fury and vengeance on "Nightline." I suppose it's futile to wait for someone to say in public what's plain, which is that these people mean no good at all, either to Jesus or the sinners he loved; their Jesus avenges everything and redeems nothing, he is a Jesus of judgment rather than mercy. They've taken their lessons from Paul as portrayed in the picture by Harry Dean Stanton, his sermon replete with the intonations and cadences of a good fundamentalist hater, who informs Jesus that he has long since given way to the Jesus that Paul and the others have invented to take his place. Fifty years ago on another continent the Falwells and Wildmons and Hymerses wore black bands around their arms as they stoked the same fires to burn the art of the damned; that the bands are now white and worn around their necks doesn't alter their truest intentions. In the summer of 1988 the most compelling man of all time has risen again after all, and he's protected by security guards with walkie-talkies who stand in the front of the theaters next to the screens to make sure no one defaces him. He's an in-your-face Jesus, a Jesus of the nuclear imagination, for whom the abyss is the body of Mary Magdalene, the denial of which binds his divinity to his humanity even as it divides the two.

To: His Excellency Haile-Mariam, Office of the President, Addis Ababa, Ethiopia. Your Excellency: I am writing to request the release from prison of Namat Issa and her son, Amonissa. Namat Issa is an Oromo civil servant who was arrested with her husband seven years ago for reasons that have never been given. Her son, Amonissa, was born behind prison walls, where he contracted a viral infection which has left him mentally retarded. At the age of seven he's never lived a day outside prison or had a moment of normal childhood; he's utterly innocent. He's the victim of political struggles of which he knows nothing, for which he cannot be held accountable; contrary to the moral dicta of ideology he is part of no solution or problem. It would be a gesture of humanitarian concern on the part of your government to free Amonissa and his mother. I have been advised by Amnesty International to make this plea in an unaccusatory fashion, and not as a statement of opposition to your government or your political system. I'm advised that it's better to proceed on the assumption that you will be moved by this letter, that it is in your nature to right an injustice once you understand the situation. So this is the situation now, and perhaps you'll surprise me and the rest of us by actually doing something about it. He's a little boy, you know. He's mentally retarded, living in a life frightening enough by the scrambled sense of it. Let him go. He will not bring down your government, only the wrong of his imprisonment could rot the fundaments of your system. I thank you for your attention to this matter.

To: Mohamed Siad Barre, President of the Somali Democratic Republic, People's Palace, Mogadishu, Somalia. Your

Excellency: I am writing in regards to the situation of Safia Hashi Madar, a biochemist and teacher who was imprisoned three years ago in Somalia when she was nine months pregnant. Her baby was born in jail after she was brutalized by the police and denied medical attention; her son was then confiscated from her. For nearly a year she was held incommunicado, during which time she was not told of the fate of her child, who had been placed with relatives. She has since been sentenced to life imprisonment for her participation in a nonviolent demonstration in July of 1985; she is in poor health, suffering from torture, deprived of medicine, and starving. I urge that she be given immediate medical treatment and I request that she be released as a prisoner of conscience. This would be an admirable gesture of humanitarianism on the part of your government. I have been advised by Amnesty International to make this plea in an unaccusatory fashion, and not as a statement of opposition to you or your government or your political system. I'm advised that it's better to proceed on the assumption that you will be moved by this letter, that it is in your nature to right an injustice once you understand the situation. Bastard. This is the situation. Have I been polite enough? Have I soothed your sense of supremacy to the extent that I might suggest you do something human for once? Torturer and assassin. A nine-months-pregnant woman who did nothing to you but commit a truthtelling, it's quite a stroke of your power, it's quite a manifestation of your supremacy to beat up and abuse a pregnant woman and take her child from her. Pig. Why can't I see your face, I'd like to know your face. I'd like to open you and see the slop of sewage in you that pretends to be a heart. How long have you been shitting out your heart until there was nothing left but a postintestinal drip, leaking somewhere beneath the stench of your lungs? Fucking butcher, puny fucking slug that rules battered pregnant women. There isn't enough Jesus in the universe for your likes; there isn't enough Jesus in me, anyway: it must be the Christian in me that hates you like this.

Not the Jesus, I suppose. Hope for your sake he's around when your time comes. Foul stinking turd of an excellency. I thank you for your attention to this matter.

• • •

After I've been in L.A. a week or two I'm off again. I meet up with Ventura in New Orleans. Years ago Ventura migrated from New York to Los Angeles via Austin, Texas; as a critic and columnist for L.A.'s main alternative newspaper he's one of the most famous writers in the city. I met him three years ago after he reviewed my first novel. Ventura's friendship exists in the context of a Sicilian flair for the selfdramatic, a Texan distrust of anything that doesn't ring absolutely true (which is to say anything that isn't of and from Texas), and a native New Yorker's natural disgust for any flourish that resembles a social nicety. He's in his early forties and someone described him as a mystic biker, or maybe the Cowboy Rasputin; a while ago he wrote a well-received movie called *Echo Park*, and he's just finished a big novel about a blues musician in Texas. It's controversial enough that he feels he now has to go back to Austin one more time and sort of prepare everybody. Or maybe just say his farewells.

It's now clear that I'm not going to be in New Orleans for the Republican Convention. The conscientious part of me regrets this but the rest is relieved. To be sure, I haven't pursued the matter quite as relentlessly as I did the Democrats, believing last March, on the basis of the way things looked then, that the Democrats were going to be the big story, conventionwise. But I have submitted my request to the Republicans in the form of several letters, at least one of which was delivered by special express mail, and enough phone calls that I couldn't even give an approximate number. I've explained to the Republicans that I'm writing this book. I don't expect them to know me but I am a little concerned when the sweet young Republican thing on the other end of the line curtly asks me to spell Simon and Schuster. We know at this point that we should prepare ourselves for possible disappointment. Sure enough, the Republicans send me a letter rejecting me outright. There's no explanation other than the fact they just have so many requests for credentials and that the teeny-weeny Superdome just doesn't have room for my huge space-consuming presence. It might as well be noted that it's a general Republican policy to accommodate only whatever media the party absolutely feels it has to, and what I don't fit into is not really the Superdome but that category of what it feels it absolutely has to accommodate. This book, in other words, will have no impact whatsoever on the outcome of the election, so what's in it for the Republicans to make me happy? Honestly, I can't bear them any grudges on this matter; I can even appreciate that we're clear who's on what side, and it can't be all bad that the Republicans have decided that I'm not on theirs, though this is not to say I'm necessarily on anyone else's. Yet.

That said, there is something tempting anyway about being in New Orleans during the Republican Convention. There is something tempting about mixing with a lot of anxious alcoholic Republicans wandering around Voodoo Country in the middle of August, irritable and sweltering with a cajun heat bubbling in their veins and bumping into whores and strippers and addicts and gamblers and people who appear to be without any doubt whatsoever flatout no-holds-barred Negroes. Negroes moreover with weird feathers and shit in their hair, weird clothes, black evil prayers and carnal curses on their lips, and this look in their eyes around twilight. A number of colleagues mount very convincing, even conscience-prickling arguments as to how I simply have to stay, it would be a disservice to this book and myself not to. Ventura, on the other hand, wants to go to Texas in his sixtysomething Chevrolet that was once green before it was stripped by the turmoil of travels that were supposed to resolve lives and loves beyond resolution. Also, I know that if the true reality of the Democrats' convention was a television reality, it will be even more so of the Republicans' convention; and I can rationalize it only half successfully that I should see one of these affairs from the vantage point of the people who drive cars with telephones that don't call anywhere. Though Ventura's car is not one of those, we are adept at talking to each other as though we're separated not by three feet but by a computer signal. There is, I should mention, another reason for not going to the Republican Convention. I am loath to bring it up, but it would be a fraud on my part not to. It's this: Ed Meese may be at this convention. The retiring attorney general of the United States. I hear the Republicans don't want him, but there's no evidence this has ever stopped Ed Meese before, Ed Meese is not the sort of man for whom something as trivial as the good of his party or country is going to get in the way. I'm almost sure, actually, that Ed Meese will be there, in that teeny-weeny Superdome, slamming around some night in the French Quarter; I'm bound to run into him. I've already run into Al Gore, I've already run into Gary Hart. I practically knocked Walter Mondale into the next tier of seats in the Omni. Why shouldn't I run into Ed Meese? I stay in New Orleans, I hang around the convention, I run into Ed Meese. And if I do, well, I'll beat him. I'll beat the man. I want to beat him. Not anything so grand as thrashing him with a rolled-up United States Constitution; I'll just grab whatever's nearest me. This telephone next to my typewriter. I'll just grab it and, you know, lodge the receiver end of it into his head with a squish. I don't care that he's not guilty of breaking some law; it's the special talent of Ed Meese that he's brought out the worst in me, that he's brought out the Ed Meese in me, the part that is careless of justice or what's fair, or what's due process. It's the special talent of Ed Meese that he's brought out in me something sickening, something that says: I want to hurt him. Not for his sleazy dealings, not for his political opportunism, just for what he is, and the way he's made shameful everything he's touched: I want to beat the man who said the states don't have to enforce the Bill of Rights, I want to beat the man who said that only guilty people are ever suspects, I want to beat the man who said that the hungry stand in line at soup kitchens only because the food is free. This nit of a man, this jot of a spirit: let me at him. Ten seconds is all I ask. There it is, then. I know what I've done here in the saying of this, I know how I've betrayed the trust others have given me in the saying of this. Here I took all that advance money from Simon and What's-his-name in order to buy luxury, the sordid indulgence of writing this, that I want to beat Ed Meese; there's no excuse for it. The critics will take me to task and rightly so. "Well, we had some hope for him, he might have turned out to be something. But then he *lost control.*" The publishing lawyers will have something to say about it, the phone's ringing right now from my editor: "You can't say," she'll point out, "you want to beat Ed Meese." It's dismaying. It's unprofessional, as my agent would say: there's no denying it. It's irresponsible. But it ought to be clear now, you ought to have figured out by now, that this book is an act of manifest irresponsibility; I am on a long trainride into irresponsibility. So the best I can do, as I often do, is draw the line on my obsessions, draw the line on my dark fantasies, which with every passing day seem to offend some longheld friendship or another, and say that I will not stay in New Orleans, for the sake of not my career, it's obviously too late for that, but for my country at least, and my good Republican parents who would not be happy to see their son on television beating the former attorney general, the man who made justice and Jeffersonian liberty gag lines in his own obscene patter.

We go to Texas.

Ventura's plan is to leave New Orleans before the final dim death of the thunder of electric lights in the moist Louisiana air, and head his car deep into the heart of Texas that we may be there by early evening in time to hear Butch Hancock and Jimmie Dale Gilmore sing at Threadgill's. I get up at six in the morning and shower quickly and load everything into Ventura's car; this includes Ventura's voodoo candles, each lit to thwart off this or invite that, and apparently three or four hundred tapes.

We pull out of the Quarter, pull into a service station where he attends lovingly to the car, and we're on the highway by eight. We're crossing the bridges that shoot up the bayous. I have already broached and retreated from the touchy subject of drivership: "If you ever want me to take over the wheel," I offer cheerfully, "just let me know." Ventura pales and swallows hard as though I've just asked him to hand over his private parts. We listen to many of his tapes, which we both love, and some of my tapes, which I love. Joe Ely, Creedence Clearwater, Robert Johnson, Dylan, Rosanne Cash, Butch Hancock, Springsteen, Muddy Waters, the Band, Patsy Cline, all these are common bonds, and an array of Texas music I've never heard. There's an amazing one by a woman named Traci Lamar singing with the Supernatural Family Band, mystical Texas folk music in Spanish and English; it rises like smoke to the brain from some fire you can't see down in the canyon. At any rate, from our perspective the car is fairly loaded down with danger. Ventura keeps checking the rearview mirror for cops, since the car radiates some kind of illegality or another, not to mention those riding in it. This is a very ironic set of circumstances since the truth of it is Ventura and I can count between us on one hand our major drug experiences. Mine are two with marijuana and one with hashish in Amsterdam, the most recent of which was twelve years ago, and Ventura's are more or less the same. The more exotic medicines are entirely alien to us: this cocaine business, I'm explaining to him, you do it with your nose. Ventura doesn't say anything at first, he's thinking. "Your nose?" he finally says. Like an elephant, I tell him. He stares at the road ahead in grim incredulity. Curled in the backseat, through the music and the talk, Sally sleeps.

Somewhere I stopped feeling the electricity. Somewhere everything wasn't a shock anymore when I touched it. I might assume it has to do with the landscape, I might assume it's that everything's so full of electricity we're all grounded to it; but I don't remember it in Los Angeles this last time either. So I know it's the time we're grounded to; in this hush, I travel wired to the present. In Ventura's rearview mirror someone follows. It's hours before he mentions it—near noon as we've already crossed the Louisiana-Texas border. I'm hungry. There was a McDonald's back there, I say; I'm pleased by the anticipation of lunch at McDonald's, at the way it offers no surprises, the genius of predictability. "I didn't see anything," Ventura argues. I'm telling you there was a McDonald's, I say, let's go back. Ventura considers this and sighs deeply. "Do you promise," he says, "that there was a McDonald's?" I promise. We get off Ten and head back to the last exit, where in the exact place I saw a McDonald's there is an empty lot of land on which nothing has stood in ages. "You promised," Ventura says flatly, staring at the empty land. Back on Ten he's watching the rearview mirror again, and after a few minutes says, "This blue Dodge has been behind us since New Orleans." For a while this sinks in on both of us. It's odd, since we got off Ten and went back a mile and a half: maybe, I suggest, someone else is having McDonald's hallucinations. I turn in the seat to determine Ventura isn't having a hallucination, but he says, "Don't turn around. *Never* turn around." *Who lives* Sally says, dazed, out of her sleep. After a while we come to a real McDonald's, one all of us can see, and we get off the highway and eat. We read a *USA Today* in the middle of nowhere, only the arches and the kids' rides in front of the restaurant interrupting the plains that will get a lot flatter after we go through some hill country outside Houston. Forty-five minutes later we're back on the road that takes off from Ten heading toward Austin, with not a blue Dodge in sight for at least five miles; and then Ventura says, "There he is again." Ventura slows in his lane and the car behind us slows, then Ventura picks up speed and the car accelerates. By four we're in Austin; and we watch the Dodge continue on down the highway, disappearing into the West and our relieved indifference, which is destined to be temporary. . . .

Austin lands on the memory with a wet smack and then seeps outward until the memory is something longer or even

without time at all. The first night we're at Threadgill's. To hear
Ventura on the subject, everything about Austin is better than
anything anywhere else; interestingly I haven't seen evidence that
he's wrong. The girl who sits us at our table is apparently one of
the ten most beautiful women in Texas, which is to say one of the
eleven or twelve most beautiful in America, but all the girls are
like this in Austin, it's beauty so manifest and everyday common-
place that neither man nor woman can use it with a guile. The
guys who wander in, like Butch Hancock and Jimmie Dale
Gilmore, shake my hand like they've been waiting their whole
lives just to meet me; and after a while the place is full without
seeming crowded. The waiter or waitress takes your order without
ever keeping tabs; at the end of the night he'll ask you what you
had and the two of you will sit there ten minutes trying to
reconstruct what you ate and drank and you'll arrive at whatever
sounds reasonable to both of you. When Hancock and Gilmore
sing, everyone listens in a fashion neither rude nor rapturous,
people will get up and walk around and visit with their friends
and then listen a little more to the music and then talk some
more, regarding Hancock and Gilmore as nothing more than the
friendly legends they are in this town. Gilmore is one of the most
beautifully mournful singers I've ever heard and Hancock has
apparently written about forty-nine percent of all the great songs
of the last fifteen years. We leave Threadgill's seven hours after
we got there having seen the evening through from beginning to
end, Sally is nowhere to be seen. She always shows up sooner or
later, I tell Ventura. We have a place to stay in Austin, an old
warehouse converted by a friend of Ventura's into living accom-
modations, a friend with a weird and incendiary political past
which I won't go into here. The warehouse has its failings. The
water from the shower has an odd odor and there are winged
cockroaches somewhat smaller than pigeons that fly out from
beneath the living room table. There's a bathroom in the middle
of the house where you can never get to it and an unattached
toilet seat that zips around the floor so much you have to take a

Dramamine to sit on it. Upstairs there are guns under my bed and in the morning you wake to the sound of a train loud enough you expect it to roll through the window. In fact the train passes right underneath the window, not twenty feet away. Ventura downstairs is sitting on the backyard porch literally watching a duck lay eggs against the other wall. We discuss in semiserious fashion the prospect of leaving the warehouse for the antiseptic motel room of our dreams, but the warehouse's aesthetic over-comes the functional defects, though in the final analysis inertia decides the issue as much as anything. We get in the car and put on a tape and go have huevos rancheros at this restaurant Ventura explains is better than any restaurant anywhere except for thirty or forty others in Austin, and then we drive along the river and through the town with its tall, empty towers. They're office buildings built to accommodate the fruits of the Reagan recovery but the funny thing is the Reagan recovery sort of rotted in Texas and now these huge glassy buildings are vacant but for the windows of Texas sky, the only big building that meant much around here in the last twenty-five years was the tower on the university where sometime in the Sixties a guy climbed to the top with a rifle and did his Robert Dole routine. Everyone still hears the shots, especially those who were never here. We go see Butch Hancock who shows us the photos he took of Russia when he went there and then to a record shop where I find Hancock and Marce Lacouture's *Yella Rose*, the great lost album of the Eighties and the album Dylan wanted *Desire* to be except it wasn't as good, music of dislocated gypsy passion. At night we go have dinner and hear Hancock again with a rock and roll band and then we tour around Austin, around the edges where there's that dark envelopment of night which shrouds only desert towns or tropical islands. . . .

Days or weeks or months later we leave Austin. Sally has been gone for some time, though if she has not found who she's looking for I know we'll see her again, hitchhiking somewhere on the highway or maybe knocking at the motel door one night as

Ventura and I are sitting inside drinking his Black Bush Irish whisky. On the way out of Austin Ventura makes his voodoo run. There's a little shop on the outskirts of town just as you're leaving; there's nothing interesting-looking about it at all from the outside, it could be a real estate office. In fact, in its way it *is* a real estate office. Voodoo's on sale inside. Strange postcards and spiritual items, candles burned to this saint or that sentiment, wax in layers of color like geological charts of the soul, in bottles painted with bright icons. Ventura walks in, looks at the candles, says I'll take that one. He doesn't mean one candle, he means one *shelf* of candles. I'll take these too, he says, indicating another two or three dozen from the next shelf. When the shop owner learns we're on our way to Los Angeles she informs us about the big earthquake that's coming, this is the word from another world or vision. She says it neither as melodrama nor advice; it's information, imparted as information, with the rationality of information, and Ventura receives this information as information, with the same rationality. We now load two or three boxes of voodoo candles into Ventura's car and we're on our way to L.A. for the Big Quake. We're heading up into the Panhandle, to Lubbock and a small town northeast of it called Clarendon. In the late afternoon the silver light of the Panhandle is roughly similar to what light will look like in the last hour of time. The earth is erratic, flat one moment and then suddenly carved in slashing red crevices: see there, Ventura points as we drive, the land is shimmering. He's right. See there, he points to a herd of cattle in the distance, the cows glow. He's right, they do. Everything is soaked with electricity now, man and metal are of like currency. See there, Ventura says, and he points to the occasional farmhouses, one every ten or twelve miles, isolated on the flat silver Texascape, little houses with small fences, little doors, a small shed to the side, and in the backyards looming huge over the houses and sheds are satellite dishes. They've all got them now, every little farmhouse in the Panhandle has a satellite dish. People living out here for years, never seeing anyone, stuck by their own design in 1952 or 1945 or 1938, where nothing has happened to their lives since, and then the dishes came, erected in a wave, and then through these dishes came the world. Through them, soaring in like through a wind tunnel, came the future. People who have known nothing but the Panhandle and a given moment in the last fifty years suddenly watching Tibetan monks in China, visions of Mars, the slaughter of seals in Canada, strangers performing sex acts. It all came in like a rush through the new round windows of the Panhandle. On upward we drive. In the distance people sit on the porches of their houses like sailors navigating their boats, sailing their houses across the Texas plains, eyes fixed on seas no one knows. Back and forth before us, crisscrossing each other's paths, the houses of the Panhandle sail, their satellite dishes full of wind. In Lubbock we stay with a woman named Deborah in a house full of God and suburban reassurances. It isn't so different from the San Fernando Valley twenty years ago except it isn't a valley: the San Fernando Valley as if, one morning, one woke to find the surrounding mountains gone. Ventura takes my picture in front of the statue of Buddy Holly. Clarendon is two hours away; we stay with Ventura's friends George and Dixie. The house was bought by George many years ago; since then he has, uh, made some adjustments in it. Driving up in twilight it appears like Cubism pushed beyond its own premises, as defined by whatever logic you can figure. Little rooms on the upper floor jut out into nowhere, long passages head south for the winter, architectural adjuncts explode without warning. "Nice house, before I got to it," says George. The stairway in the middle of the living room rises to a level that isn't completely there, the kitchen is found by following Escher-like steps that circle into themselves. The stretch between Lubbock and Clarendon is known as Saucer Alley. Everybody has seen something extraordinary in this country, though all are reluctant to discuss it because they have their pride and don't need to indulge the condescending amusement of outsiders who will say they're crazy. It strikes me that not a single one of anyone I've met in Texas is crazy with anything but inspiration. This is a difficult place. It's difficult to fathom much excitement in the part of the United States that lies between Austin and Clarendon for anyone as banal as George Bush or Michael Dukakis. And weeks or months or years after leaving it, it's only then that the blue Dodge can drive back into our lives, crossing the Red River on the highway to New Mexico when Ventura looks one afternoon into the small window that shows him his past wedged into the large window that shows us our future. I don't believe it, he says; after all we've seen, it's a blue Dodge of all things he can't believe. I turn to look now. Don't turn around, he says, you *never*—"Yeah, yeah," I say. Through the dust of our drive I squint to make out the two people in the blue Dodge: "Holy shit." What? Ventura says. "Just drive," I say. Who is it? he says. "Just drive." All I can think is, The guy's never going to forgive me for his not becoming vice president of the United States. "We'll see if they're still with us by the time we get to Santa Fe," I explain, though I already know they will be.

• • •

To: The Honorable Albert Gore, Jr., United States Senator, Interstate Ten Outside Santa Fe, New Mexico. Dear Al: There comes a point in every relationship when matters need to be clarified before the relationship is allowed to proceed too far on the basis of misunderstanding. For our relationship, this is that point. After New Mexico, after all, there is Arizona; and after Arizona, California. After California there's only the Big Wet, Al. Unless you and the Tipper plan to drive us into the sea it makes sense to call a truce here and now. I did not sabotage your vice-presidential candidacy, I'd just like to say that first off. Think about it, it makes no sense. The vice presidency would have been no good for you anyway, and Dukakis' choice of Bentsen plays right into your hands since if Dukakis is elected Bentsen will be too old to succeed him and if Dukakis is defeated you will not be tainted with the defeat. So things have worked out rather for the best, in that regard. But the second thing I wanted to tell you, and I certainly hope you don't think I would say this just because you and the wife have been chasing us halfway across the Southwest, the second thing I wanted to tell you is, well, I'm sorry, sort of. I know I've implied, well, I know I've more or less stated flat out an opinion to the effect that you're an artificial person who has constructed a facade entirely designed for the purpose of pleasing the American voter, I guess it's true that I've said rather explicitly that you're the sort of individual whose entire youth has been dedicated to currying the favor of grownups who would then see in you some lost opportunity of themselves and thus reward you with unspeakable power, but I just wanted to tell you that you are *not* the phoniest human being in public life. It's recently come to my attention that there is someone even more soulless than yourself, someone even more craven in the mechanical tinkerings of ambition, for whom nothing but ambition can justify the thesis of his candidacy, not even intelligence; I never said, after all, that you were stupid. Now there is someone on the scene even less authentic than yourself, someone beyond the zombi pale, which is one way of saying that the other political party from your own has seen fit to nominate him for vice president of the United States. Thus we might conjecture that your own hopes for the vice presidency were upended either by the fact you're not dim enough for the job, if you wish to look at it that way, or that the presidential candidate of your party was not dim enough to choose you, which is the way I wish to look at it. Either way however I have no choice but to reassess you upward. So get off my back, Al. This relentless pursuit is pointless; check the blue Dodge in at Albuquerque and take a flight back to Nashville in the morning. Take your squirrelly wife with you or leave her in the desert if that sounds better, it's our secret, eat this letter and no one will ever be the wiser. Go home, Al. It wasn't your year. We'll be back in L.A. one of these days and that's my territory; you're not near strange enough for it. You haven't mastered the hundred zones into which I can disappear only to reappear somewhen and somewhere else: I've been doing it for years. I see such points from blocks away, I got my wristwatch from Anarchy Inc. Goodbye Al, do yourself a favor. You're better than that other guy, take solace in that and walk away while you still have the chance. Who knows, someday, maybe even next Leap Year, it may be you against him. Who knows, someday, the way things are going, you might be _our best hope_. Then the place and its days will be your territory, and I won't be near strange enough for it. Yours, Steve Erickson.

• • •

Thomas. My knife chimes in the moon. A hundred nights in the dead of night I held it to your throat as you slept, you knew didn't you. You were awake all the time. Did you trust I wouldn't do it, or did you hope that I would: but what would they have written about you then. You must have wondered to yourself how the spray of your blood would have blotted your mark in history, or perhaps how it would have only deepened your legend. By then you knew you had made yourself into one of the world's great men. All these things you thought to the song of the knife: it sang to you: and leaning over your throat, naked in your bed, I meant to think nothing at all. I meant to heed the growl of my womb for something savage, in the echo of which I would only belong to you more. Thomas. I put the knife away, back under the pillow where you've known it's been all along. Great man killed by his black lover they'd have said. I think you said all along, Do it then, run your songful blade's edge across my throat that history will see the lesson of how I failed myself, that I might not be hungry for your thighs. Thomas. 1826. They tell me you're dead. The doctor comes from the room, he calls me madame. He's gone, madame. I know different, doctor, I say back to him: he cocks his head in confusion.

I know different: Jefferson lives. Twelve years later the rumor comes back to me in my own words, in a tavern in North Carolina, on a latesummer night when a farmer who's lost his harvest, drunken in the tavern and beseeched by his woman not to drink himself to death, despairing of the way his dream has gone, says in the night through the liquor, Van Buren is president, but Jefferson lives. Every other desperate face in the tavern looks up at the words, every hopeless eye lights up with faith. 1847 I hear it again. I live by the railroad tracks outside Atlanta, I prowl the night with my blade. I am paralyzed by the decision whether to answer its song with a white throat or black, when the man I've spent my night with says it in his sleep. 1866 in the ashes of Georgia. 1906 on the shores of Lake Pontchartrain. I hear it so often, my own rumor coming back to me through the lips of so many worthless mouths that would taste me, that I come to believe it's only the wicked ring of the jewels in my ears. Wicked jewels he gave me in Paris, that bled from my ears from Paris to America when I stabbed my ears with them, jewels in my ears that went on bleeding day after day, then week after week, then month after month. Across the years these small silver masks on scepters that pierced my lobes; and when they told me he was dead only then did the bleeding stop, and only then did they begin to whisper back to me my own rumor. Rumors from the open throats of men at my side, up through their mouths, past their lips, and then repeated in whispers through the tiny silver mouths of tiny silver masks in the lobes of my ears until I couldn't take it any longer. Until I tried to rip them from my ears with the same violence I'd put them there: but no such rumor could be ripped from the air. He lives. I went on wearing his cursed jewelry. 1925 north to Michigan, 1934 west to Chicago. I live with a bookseller near the university, it's not so easy to find an owner. It's not so easy to find one whose light shines bright enough that the remaining dark of him is black enough to own me: they're men queasy in their ownership. The bookseller is particularly pathetic. After a year I go to him one night and with the knife at his throat I ask, Who lives. He wakes with such a frightened start I think his heart will kill him before I do. Who lives, I ask him. He's peering around the dark of his room as though it's a foreign country, the sound of the knife at his throat has changed everything he knows. I say, Isn't there a man who understands the law? Isn't there a man who understands that the owner is as bound to the slave as the slave is to the owner? Now the rumor fades. Now headed into the whitehot core of the Twentieth Century they can't remember his name. Who lives? They might as well answer Adolf, they might as well respond Josef. Who lives. In the dark, naked against this pathetic bookseller, I could slit his throat but then go on slitting the throats of every man in America, waiting for the answer. What if none of them remembers. What if none of them knows the answer. Courage fails, vision fails. I leave him unslashed, I free myself of him, this poor feeble freedom. 1940. St. Louis, just east of the river. These are the nights of history. I live with the Historian in his house within river's view, he is a large redheaded man for whom history rides on the point of the clock's second hand. He does not go to history, history comes to him. It's Leap Year. He disappears into the upper room each twilight and reappears some time past midnight with the result of his efforts: "Tonight," he may say, "I began a war. Tonight," he may say, "I assassinated a man in Mexico. Tonight," he may say, "I divided matter in two." Each day telegrams come to our door, by a boy dressed in blue on a bicycle. History sends the big redheaded man queries in telegrams, waiting for him to write the course of events in pages to be given to the messenger the following day, and taken back into the horizon by bicycle. Five years this continues. "Tonight," he says tonight, "I dropped a bomb." Who lives? I ask in terror. "The abyss," he answers. The next day the messenger takes the new history, he returns that night white like a ghost. The messenger has never come before at night. He has the pages of the new history given to him that morning still in his hands, he holds them out from himself at arm's length to give them back. He stands on the *porch of the house, the river dark behind him in the Kansas night to the west. The Historian stands large in the door. The messenger shakes his head and tries to find the words. "We . . . beg you not to," he tries to explain to the Historian, "not this." I've dropped a bomb, the Historian only repeats, it's all right, it's an American bomb. "Not this," the messenger repeats, shaken, "we beg you not to." Then, the Historian answers, go find the ones who will accept such a history. They're out there, I assure you of that; they're out there waiting for just this particular history, for just this particular bomb. They're out there waiting for just this particular event by which all the history that's come before is pulled free of its time, like written words from under which the page is pulled. Words that have nothing against which to lay themselves, that's the history I've written tonight. It's my best history yet, the redheaded Historian nods certainly. He closes the door in the messenger's face. Together we listen to the whine of the bicycle vanishing. We never hear it again. The messenger never returns. The Historian is left to write his unread history for only himself. He sits among the pages of history waiting for a messenger. I leave seven weeks later. 1955–1968. Montgomery Little Rock Atlanta Birmingham Dallas Selma Los Angeles Harlem Chicago . . . Sometimes I dream of returning to Paris if it's not too late. Everyone always thinks of going back to the place where they made their most important choice, the desire is strongest when they suspect their choice was wrong. The desire is strongest when they suspect their choice was wrong but if they had the choice to make again they would make it the same wrong way. Now I'm in the backseat of a car skinned of its green shell, two men are in the front. Through the window of the car is a sky blown out at its edges, like a huge unfolded blue flower. My eyes drown in it, my jewels whisper no more rumors. One of the earrings has been gone some months now, I noticed it missing in New Orleans when I saw Thomas on the ghost car that rolled free of its train up the tracks of the St. Charles Trolley. Saw him in the window and then when I got to the cabin it was the same as always. Sometimes I dream of returning to Paris. My vision from the backseat of this car, lying flat on the seat staring upside down into the sky, my vision falls into it. I rub the torn part of my lobe. The man driving has long hair pulled back and tied behind him, his passenger seems familiar. I rode with him on a train not long ago, perhaps; perhaps we've spoken of things. Did he say it to me once? though we've never been together. Did he say the rumor. Did I hold the blade once to his neck, on a train or in an empty lot outside a concert hall. But now I sense something around the next bend. Now I sense I should sleep here, not as the slave of these men, these men are already the slaves of their dreams. These men are only beginning to wake, halfway through their lives, to what's shattering and unkind about the truth. Sometimes I dream of returning to Paris. The edges of red mountains creep in around the upside-down window of my vision, I sense something around the bend. I sense something in the mountains at the edge of what I see. The passenger is a man with more secrets than he can stand to believe, I long ago learned to tell everyone my secrets. Sometimes I dream of returning. . . . When I wake again it's dark. The men have left me to sleep in the open car. It's dark, my vision holds no edges at all. It's dark, I do not have a rumor to share. I touch my torn ear: who lives, I say to the dark empty inside of the car. I was the slave of the man who made America, and now America is the slave of me. Who lives. Sometimes I dream of returning. I hear no rumor. My torn ear is empty, no rumor speaks to it. Who lives. From far out in the dark, before I fall to sleep once again, the only answer is the whine of the bicycle, the only sight that crosses the edges of my black vision are the telegrams of history fluttering in the night, thrown like confetti.*

• • •

You believe in secrets Sally says *you talk of secrets all the time.* As summer turns to fall the heat of the country follows us west; on

Labor Day weekend Los Angeles records its hottest day ever. The drought of Iowa and the Dakotas gives way to the infernos of Wyoming and Montana; and at our backs with Texas in its sights is the most monstrous hurricane of the Twentieth Century. *"Tonight," he might say, "I divided matter in two. Tonight," he might say, "I dropped a bomb."* There's no denying that it may be before all this my spirit wilts; but I don't believe the answer's that easy. My spirit wilts before so many things it seems impossible it will revive anytime soon: the news is full of rebellion. The rebellion of the earth, the rebellion of the sea. The rebellion of the sun and sky. These things rebel against us; the planet's had enough of us. The earth, says Ventura, is scratching its fleas. All that's left is to side with the earth and sea and sun and sky, and rebel against ourselves. George Bush is an environmentalist now. I know because I saw it on the network news: right there, he said it. "I'm an environmentalist." This must be startling news if you happen to be the environment. The government of which Bush cannot quite decide whether he was ever a part has shown the earth and sky the most brutal neglect of any United States government in memory: but so what. The press does not call Bush on this matter, they're too busy congratulating the brilliant tactic of seizing the issue of earth and sky on the piers of Boston Harbor. Everything in American politics has become a tactic, and if the tactic is a lie that works then it's a brilliant tactic. The lies cross the land in latitudes and longitudes and America has just become a secret, something utterly distinct and different in all its secret forms, and something bearing no resemblance at all to the original secret of it. We can only wonder what secret America George Bush carries in him, what secret America Michael Dukakis carries, or whether either of them has a secret America at all. The legacy of Ronald Reagan who has transformed America into a television event is that, as with all television events, two things have been rendered essentially illusory: the truth of what's happened, and one's involvement with it. Reagan's success has been analyzed over and over as that of someone who believed clearly in clear values, and that's because he made those values and that conviction clear in terms of how television conveyed them. The actuality of what happened under Reagan is impertinent, and we can sneer at Reagan's unspoken contention that wishing something makes it so, but in an era of ubiquitous images and information over a dizzying cosmos of media outlets, that contention is borne out at least until the consequences of mindboggling debt and the illiteracy of seventeen-year-olds graduating underfunded schools and the rebellion of a planet that's sick of us come washing over us like the garbage of the ocean. It's cynical but things have gotten to the point where just identifying the cynicism is naive. Now the people in the George Bush campaign are taking this cynicism to a new place. People like Lee Atwater and Roger Ailes and James Baker and John Sununu and Stuart Spencer are not really Reaganesque, they're Nixonian as informed by Reaganesque lessons. They stop at nothing to accomplish what they want to accomplish, and if they run a campaign this way, they'll run the country this way too. They understand they're living in a new age which, personified by Reagan, gives them the means to stop at nothing, not simply the political and technological means but the ethical means as well. They invent whole psychiatric pasts for Michael Dukakis, they have Kitty Dukakis burning the American flag in some distasteful and imaginary history, and between the two Dukakises, the Greek and the Jew, the Bush campaign and its "unauthorized" surrogates insinuate a hatred of the flag which is to say a hatred of America. This truth is embodied in the Bush argument over the Pledge of Allegiance, and Dukakis' apparent view of an America in which one is not compelled by the state to take such oaths. It's a shrewdly vicious stroke on Bush's part and Dukakis is powerless against it; the press ridicules Dukakis for presenting a constitutional rebuttal to Bush's charge, and of course the press is right. How uninteresting and untalented of

Dukakis that the best he can come up with is reason and history in the face of a brilliant tactic. When Bush waves the flag all Dukakis can wave back is the First Amendment, when anyone could tell him that Americans don't much like the First Amendment. We've had no use for it now for many years, neither on the Left nor the Right; we believe only in its effective protection of our own point of view or the status quo. The First Amendment's popularity has long since collapsed before the Fire In A Crowded Theater argument, though I personally have never heard anyone cry fire in a crowded theater. I was even in a theater once that caught on fire, and nobody cried fire there either, rather an usher calmly informed us the place was burning down and we might wish to leave. I have on the other hand heard of people around the world imprisoned or tortured or executed by the status quo which was offended by their expression, and of countries where people who don't take oaths of allegiance are criminals, but those people and places aren't as interesting as Americans sitting in crowded theaters worried that any moment someone's going to cry fire, or Americans sitting in crowded halls worried that someone's not going to pledge allegiance to the flag, which actually once stood for something other than George Bush's shabby and selfcongratulatory love for a country the fundamental raison d'être of which he despises and holds in contempt. Thus the empty place in George Bush where there should be a secret America may well be the empty place America has become; we'll find out in November, when Americans make a choice between Dukakis and his vapidness, Dukakis, who given his immigrant roots probably does have a secret America but who for the sake of his political fortunes has buried it so deeply one wonders if he'll be able to dig it up again in the event he does become president, and George Bush and the small mean America that he's placed with surprising skill in the empty place of him where there's no America at all, the America where more than in any election in my lifetime a major presidential candidate has drawn a naked line in the ground and said, Those on my side are patriots and those on the other are not. And by the terms of the new patriotism, Bush is right, by the terms of the patriotism of the United States, those on the other side are not patriots: and there I am. There I am left with the dreadful and crushed fact which is that it isn't the United States I love, it's America. And it went somewhere, like a crazed gene of me that's always in my body but never in my moment, which is to say I can only hope sometime in my life I will step into that moment where that gene in me waits. This new patriotism, by which some unfamiliar thing the new patriots call America is judged by what's owned and how much damage can be done, has in George Bush the perfect spokesman, perfect for the way he has, by all accounts, by even the testimony of people who like him, never believed in anything, perfect for the chameleon truth of him, adaptable on a moment's notice, scrapping shreds of things that resemble principles in the blink of the mind's eye, and assuming new ones. We won't call Bush a political whore because it insults whores; a whore engages in an honest business transaction, the pleasure of her for the money of you. We won't bother searching for striking images or terminology for characterizing Bush; we'll just simply say he's a liar and leave it at that, except to note how his lies are aimed at what's ugly and little in people. Those who profess his personal decency can keep it, it may be a decency that impresses the Connecticut crowd, the money crowd who can afford to buy and sell so many commodities they just naturally assume the truth is among them. It's perhaps only the most sickening of any number of sickening things about this campaign that George Bush, the man who believes in nothing, is running as the man who believes in something; and that Michael Dukakis, who from his history can reasonably be assumed to believe in something, has decided his best recourse is to run as the man who believes in nothing. It's the paradox of our political times that our new metaphors have found life in these slight vessels, Bush and

Dukakis, who somehow are not real enough to lead as men but not fascinating enough to lead as metaphors, such as Ronald Reagan who was complete metaphor, nothing about him by the end of his days real at all, not a word he says, not a thought he thinks, not a gesture he makes, not a value he espouses, not a conviction he evinces, nothing but metaphor. The most startling expression of this paradox is the Republican vice-presidential candidate, who has become a metaphor for my own youth, and the youth of my peers—for my, they insist, generation. This is undoubtedly the sweet revenge of those who most hate my generation. Dan Quayle is an older person's idea of a younger person. I don't know a member of my generation who within three minutes of watching him doesn't get sick to his or her stomach; he's every snot we ever knew in high school and college, his nose so fertilized from shoving it up the ass of every figure of authority who could give him something that you could grow little plants out of it if you wanted, a daffodil maybe, a potted palm. More disgusting is the apparent success of this obsequiousness: having done nothing to warrant admission to college, he was admitted to college; having done nothing to warrant admission to law school, he was admitted to law school; having done nothing to warrant graduation from law school, he was graduated from law school; having done nothing to warrant election to Congress, he was elected to Congress; having done nothing to warrant election to the Senate, he was elected to the Senate; having done nothing to warrant nomination to the vice presidency, he has been nominated to the vice presidency. Should we actually elect him to the vice presidency I trust we won't compound the insult by actually supposing he thereby warrants our respect. Never having taken a stand of his own against whichever grownup, from his father to his father's friends to George Bush, could advance his interests, he never grew up; and as the ultimate manifestation of Videamerica, chosen by Ailes and Atwater, men of a nastiness so proud they revel in it in the pages of newsmagazines, this Quayle is somehow the appropriate trigger of a national examination the likes of which must be incomprehensible to him, since there's no indication he's ever applied the smallest process of examination to himself, and there are a number of indications to the contrary. This utterly superficial human being has become the living time tunnel back to a decade, the Sixties, which smart political chic now finds expedient to trash; and to be sure there's a fair amount that invites trashing. This examination is also attended to with some guilt, which has to do with the Vietnam War and those who didn't fight in it, and why; often it's the facile guilt of the man who, by circumstance or luck or timing, happens to miss boarding the plane that goes on to crash somewhere between airports. The man feels guilty for not being on the plane. Others have written about this guilt with misplaced eloquence. Not me. I am not flippant about the fact that I didn't fight in Vietnam, and certainly I am not more moral for it; but it was not a good war. I thought I'd mention this to the generation before us that called us cowards for not wanting to go there and to the generation after us that watches its exploits in movie theaters and think it looks cool. We weren't going off to stop Hitler. By 1969, which was the year of truth for both Quayle and myself, no one thought it was a good war, and after some six years of that war, while one may have been ambivalent about many of the arguments waged over it, no one had heard an especially persuasive argument in explanation of it other than that Lyndon Johnson didn't want to be the first president to lose a war. Who wanted to die for Lyndon Johnson's ego, or for the ego of the president who followed him? My dilemma was resolved by a number, 345, my draft lottery number, which I still remember, as well as remembering the night the lottery was conducted and how I was waiting on tables at the time, and who told me the number and when and where; this will attest, if you need such testimony, to the way Vietnam hung over everyone. Doom or

salvation was drawn from a barrel of numbers and matched with
our birthdays. Even if you were born in Leap Year they had a
number for you. Quayle was not as lucky as I numberwise and
went into the National Guard. I don't care about it. I don't care
that he went into the National Guard, I don't care that he went
in to get out of fighting in Vietnam. I don't care if he pulled a
hundred strings to do it. Every guy I knew would have pulled
whatever strings he could to keep out. But if I should happen to
run into the honorable senator, and I'll recognize him by all the
daffodils in the middle of his face, I'll have this to say to him:
wave no flags in my face, man. Don't tell me how someone else
is soft on communism, or I'll have to beat you like I beat the
attorney general of the United States. I did beat the attorney
general of the United States, didn't I? I don't remember now.
The memory of it is somewhere on the other side of Weird
Texas, with Hurricane Gilbert riding in on the surf and flying
saucers zooming around in between. The sad truth of my own
vietnamed youth is that I was a coward all around, not guilty you
understand for not being unlucky enough to be sent, but because
if they had called me I would have gone, I would not have had
the nerve to buck the system, or the clarity of conviction or, most
of all, the cruel courage to break my parents' hearts. Canada was
never in the picture, I never even considered it: I hoped it was a
moral dilemma I would not have to face; and I didn't. In terms
of heroism, heroes were the ones who went and died, we know
that; the war was not noble but that does not negate the nobility
of those who died for something bereft of nobility: they died for
their own nobility. There was the heroism of those who went to
jail, making a different choice and manfully facing the system's
consequences; whether one agrees or not with the choice, these
people were true to themselves. Not even in the equation of
heroism are young militarists who joined the National Guard to
get out of fighting while rooting for the real soldiers and now
bemoaning the alleged weakness of a country that doesn't flex its

muscles often enough to excite them. George Bush shouting on
television about how proud he is of Quayle's not going to Canada
is too nauseating to abide; but you know, maybe it's just the heat.
Maybe I'm just not thinking straight. Maybe like everyone I'm
sucked into perspectives that don't matter, before the rebellion of
the earth and sea, the sun and sky; the earth doesn't care about
Dan Quayle. The earth doesn't care about phony patriots, the
earth doesn't care about the United States at all. The earth has its
own agenda now, the sun has its own priorities. It's cooking the
hell out of us, and a decade from now, if this drought continues
and becomes a chronic reality rather than some aberrational solar
whim, the earth isn't going to care when the United States,
having already lost its industrial base to Japan and West Germany, watches its agricultural base go up in smoke too, stalks of
corn smoldering like torches across the farmlands, their tops the
yellow of fire rather than food; the earth isn't going to care much
about how none of the world's major banks belong to the United
States anymore, or how the United States owes a debt the world
won't tolerate anymore, or how the United States is suddenly a
nation with Third World resources even as its residents have
come to define Americanism in terms of First World consump-
tion. Then they're going to come for us, the earth and its people,
the long death march to America, as someone put it to me; and
what will we have to hold them back but another fifty MX
missiles that no one can figure out how to deploy anyway, and
someone like George Bush who wakes every morning to a new
day of finding a new way of proving his political masculinity.
That's what will be there to protect us. Once we would have had
something else, once we would have had this: once we would
have said, But this is America, and we're Americans. And it
might have meant something, because the most resonant and
astonishing thing about America was that no matter how often it
failed its own promise, the promise was still unshakable, and for
that promise millions chose to come here; they're not flocking to

Russia, after all. They're not flocking to Poland or China or Cuba. The light of the promise, like the light of a star that died far away, outraces the alchemy of image and communication by which the phony patriots transform their contempt for what was difficult and passionate about America into the stuff of pure political power; and too much bad policy and bad faith by the Left over the years helped them do it. So that's my secret. Sally has no use for my secrets. That's my secret, the secret of our acquiescence; it's our fault, George Bush is not to account for it. Let's not blame him, he's not ever been big enough for that much blame, a glorified office boy for twenty-five years who never did an important thing in his whole political life except learn how to say Yes sir in eighteen different languages, someone who was born to do someone else's bidding and then to have his own office boy, handpicked by his pollster and media man that a generation of office boys might follow them. It actually is rather appropriate that these office boys should be president and vice president, we deserve them, and we deserve the consequences of them. Tonight on television, in a program about Republican post–World War Two presidents, I see the editor of *The Wall Street Journal* saying that while he can forgive Richard Nixon for Watergate, he can't forgive him for his imposition of wage and price controls in 1971; his sense of social outrage, in other words, is stirred by economic regulation but not by the attempted destruction of the United States Constitution. Today in a newspaper I see a new poll regarding people's feelings about the Pledge of Allegiance; not only do seventy percent of them believe the state should have the power to force someone to take the Pledge of Allegiance, but at least half of them favor this even if it's unconstitutional. So there you have it. Wave goodbye to your country with the hand that isn't busy throwing it away. We're a nation of traitors now, worse than the spies who sell secrets to the Russians. We've traded the secret of the country for whichever acquisition we can't live without; let's not put it all on George

Bush. It's us. We've abandoned the danger of our secrets in the way the earth's abandoned its merciful affection for us, in the way God created the amazing New Mexico mountains outside my window and then, having done so, scared himself, and left. We made America and scared ourselves, and left.

• • •

After eight months the Internal Revenue Service has ended their investigation of my 1985 taxes. The basic facts of the case, regarding the accuracy and honesty of my general income as I've reported it, and the accuracy and honesty of my general deductions as I've reported them, were established to the government's general satisfaction within the first four weeks. The time since has been spent by the auditor on arcana, questions that have been asked over and over. One, for instance, concerns my deduction of the cost of the electric lights in the living room where I work. Is it always my hand that turns on these lights, or does the hand sometimes belong to my wife? Does she perform some sort of non-income-related activity by these same lights that might cloud the issue of their deductibility? I explain to the government for the third time that I'm using these lights to write, I don't write in the dark though I can understand it might seem that way to some people. Here's the process: I sit down, I turn on the lights, I write. In the background somewhere it is wholly possible that my wife may be doing this or that and as a result use some of this particular light. Another question regards a $22 phone bill, and whether I might legitimately deduct all or part of it; after months of this I'm ready to concede the issue. If it will make the United States happy I will write the government a check for the tax on $22. This goes on and on through the summer and autumn. I can tell from my accountant's voice on the phone the dread with which he must report the repetition of yet another already oft-answered query. The questions aren't even asked in different ways, they're always asked in the exact same way. "But, say, Mr.

Erickson, we've just noticed there's a $22 phone deduction. . . ."
I answer in the same way as well, though each time with
somewhat less charm. Apparently at no point in the last seven
months has it occurred to anyone in the IRS that this may no
longer be worth their time and affort. At no point does some
bureaucrat say, "Well, we've established that this Erickson has
no millions piled away somewhere in a secret account, and that
his records are pretty careful and we've found no reason to believe
they're out of order, and perhaps therefore we should do
something else with our time and save the taxpayers some money
and not ask him the same thing we asked three times already
about his $22 phone bill." The paranoid political fantasies of my
friends no longer seem unreasonable.

The final upshot of the business is that after eight months of
exhaustive investigation, the IRS decides I owe the government
of the United States $33. Add to this the penalty and the amount
soars to $39. I've done my own figuring, in the meantime,
beginning with the investigator on my case who's spent on it
probably a couple of hours a week at least, say, and maybe he
makes, just guessing, $17 an hour, which means he's been paid
over the course of eight months $1,150 toward the specific end of
bringing me to justice. Assuming the auditor's supervisor makes
around, I don't know, $23 an hour, and puts, what—thirty
minutes a week?—toward my case, that adds up over eight
months to $375. The secretary handling my file must make at
least eight bucks an hour, maybe spending between thirty and
forty minutes a week on the melee of paperwork recording my
wild financial doings: let's figure after eight months $175. Then
there are the computer costs, transportation costs, Xeroxing costs,
office expenses, telephone bills: what could these add up to, $15,
$20 a week? Let's go low and say $500 total over eight months.
Add all this up and we're talking $2,200, a number that's
probably, if anything, modest. It could just as well be twice that.
The government has invested $2,200 and eight months to

determine that I owe it $39; we don't need to say much more, do we? We sort of get the idea, don't we? It's during this time that Michael Dukakis announces his intention to balance the nation's budget with tougher enforcement of the tax collection laws. Sitting in a motel room in New Mexico I'm sure I hear him on TV one night say it right out. "My friends," Dukakis says, "we're going to balance this budget, first of all by collecting the billions of dollars in uncollected taxes that aren't being paid today by deadbeats like Steve Erickson." I jump off the bed at this; Ventura, sitting in a chair by the window gazing on the Santa Fe horizon through the daze of Irish whisky, turns to me. "Dukakis just said he's going to audit me again," I explain, pointing at the TV. Ventura stares at Dukakis on the TV awhile and nods at this news; he's even a little crestfallen for me, though he generally tends to think I deserve whatever I get. My whole financial arc in the last few years just couldn't have been timed worse: poor in the Reagan Era with the prospect of being better off in the Dukakis Era, I've gotten it all backward. Maybe there's something in George Bush after all; maybe, as the possibility of a more affluent future flows through my soul, I feel the surge of what Bush likes to call traditional values. If I could just get myself up into one of those Republican brackets I wouldn't have to worry about being audited, assuming there won't be a Dukakis Era at all, as it's now obvious there won't, assuming Bush is elected, as it's now obvious he will be. "Say," it comes to me, narrowing my eyes at the TV with suspicion, "I hear this guy doesn't like the Pledge of Allegiance."

My evolution into a Republican, then, takes shape as we head across the Southwest. The most striking thing is how easy it seems, the illusory triumphs of Republicanism immediately beguiling once one submits to them. I understand that most young people now consider themselves Republicans; thus the inevitability of Republicanism, the psychological offensive with which Republicanism lays siege to the future. I also understand that my peers are becoming Republican by the bushel; a friend in New York tells me on the telephone how "angry" everyone there is with Dukakis. They don't explain why they're angry with him except that he has not more forcefully dissuaded them from following their own instincts, which are to vote for Bush: thus the further inevitability of a Republicanism that lays siege to the past. There are obstacles to my Republican evolution, to be sure; my favorite song on the radio is by a band named Midnight Oil that sings, "How do we dance while the earth is turning, how do we sleep while our beds are burning?" These don't sound like Republican sentiments to me. Patti Smith's new song begins innocently enough—"People have the power" is something Ronald Reagan could have said—but the next part blows it, "to wrestle the earth from fools." Since the Republicans have been in charge they're by implication the fools from whom the earth is to be wrestled. Then there's Tracy Chapman, a revolutionary for Republicans. Chapman's a young black woman whose very political folkblues album is, incongruously, the most popular in the country. She's a talented singer and uneven writer who's not nearly as good as people want to think she is; I suspect the symbolism of her success is what people need, as well as the symbolism of her sincerity. But which people need it? Who's making this record so popular? Like those who embraced Springsteen's "Born in the USA" four years ago, shutting out the words, and then went and voted for Reagan against Mondale, those who embrace Chapman's call to revolution, such as it is, are just as likely to vote for George Bush. That decision won't be obstructed by Chapman's politics but rather will be made possible by them, social conscience satisfied with the purchase of a seven-dollar artifact, and selfinterest thus left free to vote Republican. It doesn't hurt, from the Republican perspective into which I'm easing by the moment, that Chapman's most explicitly political songs are also her least inspired and perceptive. In spite of her best intentions she's a trend now, which is to say rendered harmless, in the way a different trend meant to render Springsteen harmless. But how do we sleep while our beds are burning? says the radio in Ventura's car; and I can't bring myself to turn it off.

I ignore it in the pursuit of my basic equation. I have every reason to suspect my basic equation is a Republican one: I remember the political identity of my teens when my mother got me an interview with the 1968 Republican campaign in California. I sat in an office with a guy who kept asking me, skeptically, why I was for Nixon. I don't think I really looked or sounded to him like someone who was for Nixon, and I didn't have a past membership in the Young Republicans or anything, in the same way I never gave myself up to most of the protests that took place at UCLA where I went to school over the next few years. Too much suspended disbelief was demanded by both, too much submission to a collective thought or sentiment. I'm not sure exactly how I put it to this guy, with all the sophistication of an eighteen-year-old, but the gist was that I was for Nixon because the alternative was Lyndon Johnson's surrogate; and history, assuming it had any rationale at all, wasn't going to accept Lyndon Johnson's surrogate. There was no way we'd be able to explain it years later, given Lyndon Johnson. Now there's no way I can explain it years later, given Richard Nixon. The guy across the desk didn't know what I was talking about. What kind of reason is that? he was thinking to himself, the thought framed in his face like his head framed in the noontime window behind him, and I think he just said to himself, and maybe to my mother, in so many words, He's not to be relied on, is he. That insistence of reliability, that acquiescence to order, is one of the exhilarating things about Republicanism; there's a peace of mind about it. There's a clarity, a conciseness with which a value lends itself to television, which not only demands that values be concise but in fact dictates that if a value isn't concise enough for television, then it's too complicated to be a value.

The appeal of Barry Goldwater's conservatism, in the shadow not so much of the New Deal but Lyndon Johnson's open hunger for power, was its Jeffersonian nature, which is to say it seemed to favor the free individual before the power of centralized authority. Obviously there were issues where Goldwater was wrong and the Jeffersonian nature of his conservatism was manifested less in an emphasis on individual rights than on states' rights—his vote against the 1964 Civil Rights Act, most blatantly—but Goldwater's intellectual honesty usually held its own even in the face of a morally mistaken position. Now outside Albuquerque something troubles my Republican evolution, which has to do with the basic equation of this conservatism from which Reaganism grew. Because while both Nixon and Reagan and those around them have over the course of twenty years given lip service to Jeffersonian conservatism, they have in fact acted as Hamiltonian conservatives. Which individual freedom has Reagan ever expressed passion for? One, the freedom to make a profit. The freedom to make a profit has for Reagan warranted passion even at the expense of those individual freedoms that derive from the most human of liberties, the freedom to think. Reagan the nemesis of government power almost never speaks with force about freedom of speech unless it's purely in the abstract or in the context of communist oppression; the Reagan "conservatives" are not much bothered by the government's power to tap your phone or monitor your mail or invade your privacy; they're not much bothered by the government's power to regulate what you read or control your access to information about the government; they don't object too heatedly to the interference of the government in matters of personal behavior if that behavior offends their own personal morality; they don't sputter with much indignation about the power of the government in obstructing your right to vote, as demonstrated by Reagan's original opposition to the extension of the Voting Rights Act; they don't lose much sleep at night over the prospect of various government agencies spying on groups that peacefully and constitutionally pursue agendas different from theirs; it didn't cause the president anguish to have an attorney general who argued that state governments are not obligated to recognize the Bill of Rights as necessarily pertaining to the residents of those states; in short, Jeffersonian freedom actually elicits from these conservatives not only a lack of fervor but often derisive disdain. The sort of conservatism these lovers of individual freedom have really cared about since Goldwater is one of a Hamiltonian love of order and, more than this, a presumption that freedom extends from the state to the individual, that freedom is something the state in its benevolence allows us, even as the premise of Jefferson was the opposite, that people are born with freedoms given to them by no laws but rather God, freedom that belongs to them by virtue of no government benevolence but the simple fact that they're persons. The First Amendment gives no one freedom of speech. The First Amendment presumes that one already has freedom of speech; it says only that the state cannot take it away. This is what made Robert Bork so philosophically transparent in the confirmation hearings for his appointment to the Supreme Court. Arguing as these conservatives do that he prizes individual freedom before the power of the state, he laid out positions over the course of the hearings in which freedom was implicitly defined not as something which naturally resides in the hands and hearts of citizens but rather as something extended to individual citizens by the state in a sensible fashion. Particularly revealing was not only Bork's view of the right to privacy, on which his nomination ultimately foundered, but his interpretation of the Ninth Amendment, which says that because a right is not specified in any of the other amendments, it does not mean the government may presume that the existence of that right can be denied. It's the ultimate escape clause for the individual in his freedom from the state. Bork, queried early in the hearings about it, suggested that as far as he had ever been able to tell, the Ninth

Amendment doesn't mean anything. I don't think this was intended as an arrogant or cavalier response, but it was an unvarnished reflection of Bork's vision of the basic nature of freedom. Freedom was something, he explained over and over, of a finite quality: when it's added in this place, it's subtracted in that. On such an assumption, what is there to account for the fundamental pluses and minuses but the government? On that assumption, what does the government become but the originator of freedom, the first mathematician of its finite boundaries? The basic tendencies of men like Reagan and Meese and Bork and Bush, not even to mention Quayle and Hatch and Helms, are authoritarian; the basic tendency of the Jeffersonian, to such consternation among conservatives that they reject it, is freedom that pushes toward the anarchic. This isn't to suggest that society can exist without authority and order, or can be as free as Jefferson imagined in his dreamiest moments. It is to say that the modern conservatives are phony Jeffersonians in the same way a lot of them are phony patriots.

So you can already see my Republican difficulties. Ronald Reagan has belied and deformed the meaning of conservatism as he's posited it in its ideal form, attacking the parts of the whole he claims to champion; and this upended conservatism is only supplemented by his nonchalant fiscal recklessness as well as his personal inability ever to take responsibility for his actions. Bush has inherited all these characteristics in a manner that's possible only for someone who has no political character of his own. Ideological followers are true believers but ideological leaders are by nature opportunists, since ideology doesn't necessarily have anything to do with the truth, and when it does it's only a happy coincidence. Ideology is a system of thought coupled with an expression of faith in history, and when one or the other must give way, it's the former, not the latter. Under ideology ideas are systematically arranged toward the end that faith dictates, thoughts are invariably shaped in a way that's selective, and once

thought becomes selective, the thinker begins lying to himself.
He excludes the thought that threatens his faith, or he will
reinvent a bias once held in order to accommodate the transforming faith, like Ronald Reagan reinventing his biases about
the Soviets—which is different from actually rethinking the
matter—in order to accommodate a new view that will not
threaten the original tenets of that faith. At the farthest limit of
ideology is faith in historical destiny, without which ideology
loses its hold on the believers. The riddle of the Twentieth
Century is that, in its scientific break with so much religious
faith, it created the vacuum of belief that ideology filled, even as
the very nature of that break belied ideology as well, because of
course the Twentieth Century belied time as we know it. In so
doing it belied history as we know it. In so doing it belied destiny
as we know it. A small hole was punctured on a temporal latitude
marked 1945, and through that hole rushed the black future,
curving around on the horizon like a boomerang and then
threading the present. Einstein was the Great Anti-ideologue,
because in the way he refracted the past and present and future,
he as well subverted any destiny to which history might pretend.
When history is revealed not to be destined, the lie of ideological
faith is exposed.

Before another motel window, before another sunset, looking out the window on the lot where the car's parked, I think I see
her. She could be any age. She could be any color. It had to be
called to my attention that she was beautiful. Now through a
thousand punctures in the late 1980s, as through the windows of
satellite dishes on the Texas plains, as through the dilated single
eyes of computer terminals, information swarms through and fills
the air. Thought is both necessarily more selective and less
so—more because there is so much more to be known and
thought than we can know and think, less because it's so much
more impossible to disregard the knowledge we don't want to
know, the thought we don't want to think. The chaos of

information nearly defies policing, the Orwellian spectacle of information-control efficiently possible only when a thing to be known or thought is snuffed not just fetally, not just embryonically, but before whatever constitutes the original conception of that known or thought thing; because if it's not snuffed then, it's too late. The bloom of something known or thought might be uprooted among whole peoples, but the mere glimpsed seed of it in the mind of a single person retains a potential to grow. In a technological age it's possible for a person in China and another person in Brazil and another person in Montana instantly to know the same thing and reach the same thought about it, through computers and television; information sprays the atmosphere with itself. When the selectivity of what's believed is too anarchic for regimentation, ideology becomes a terminal case, faith is up for grabs. Faith is held less in common as information is held more in common; the dazzling variations on objective truth supplied by an infinity of known and thought things leave every person to his own subjective truth: the permutations are too crazy for anything else. The three people in China and Brazil and Montana may know and think one common thing about Thing A, but the person in China also knows and thinks one common thing about Thing B with someone in Iceland and Australia, and the person in Brazil knows another thing about Thing C with someone in Japan and Quebec; the person in Montana may know one of these things with the person in Quebec but something else with the person in Australia. The helices of an infinity of known things stagger and ultimately decimate any one overarching system of thought. The only singular instance of commonality left is a massive resistance to the nuclear imagination, which is to say the massive collective denial of the abyss which all faith and ideology deny. In the terror of the nuclear imagination which finally consumes us is ideology's last opportunity to hold people in its power.

And through a thousand punctures in the late 1980s rush

quandaries of the spirit that no system of thought or faith can claim as its to resolve by historical right. As the quandaries multiply, the vacuum of belief seems only bigger, and the ideology that becomes less true with each passing moment also becomes, with each parallel moment, only more attractive to those who need to believe. The leaders seize the opportunity of power that this need presents, but in the end the quandaries defeat them. Over the motel TV now comes news from across the land of the demonstrations at abortion centers in over thirty major American cities; besides the budget deficit, abortion remains the great issue of 1988 before which the political leaders cower. They cower because it defies ideological context, and it's cheapened in the anguished ambivalence of its argument when ideologues of both sides try to control it. No other issue so well crystallizes the futility of ideology, or the way ideology is instantly transcended by questions of soul and sex, death and birth. All that's left after the blaze of the debate is each woman as a nation unto herself, an ideology unto herself. Conservatives argue either that the fetus is an independent human life or—supposing such an argument is unconvincing to many women who, feeling the physical need of the thing that grows in them, suspect differently—that in any case, since it is not known when life may begin, the fetus deserves the benefit of the doubt. Where this logic would stop is never disclosed. An IUD sits coiled inside the woman to abort a fetus at the moment of conception; we have not yet heard this called murder. The birth-control pill aborts the biological circumstances in which life would otherwise be created; we have not yet heard this called preemptive murder. Listening to middleaged men sit before congressional committees lecturing women about the nature of birth, one finds inescapable the undertone of unforgiving wrath, which leads inescapably in turn to the feeling that much of the antiabortion movement is essentially antisex. Much of the antiabortion movement is about recrimination, the merciless twisted justice that would in some dark hearts make that sixteen-year-old girl in the backseat of the car pay for the pleasure that middleaged men both deplore and desire. Liberals hurry to their own hypocrisy. Arguing that the decision over abortion lies in the realm of individual choice, they then contend the state shall sanction the choice with a subsidy, though the state has received no consensus from the populace to do so, and to receive such a consensus and act upon it would amount to a tyranny of its own against those who sincerely oppose abortion out of moral or religious conviction. The woman who should not have the views of others imposed on her individual choice about abortion nonetheless would have the right to impose her choice on others by having them pay for her abortion. Liberals argue that if a woman indeed has a constitutional right to an abortion, as the Supreme Court decided in 1973, then to deny her funds for the abortion is an effective denial of her constitutional rights. By the same argument, one is denied the right of a free press if the government does not buy him a printing press, and one is denied the right to bear arms if the government does not buy him a gun. The liberal understanding of the Constitution is often exactly as conservatives have suggested, that the Constitution and Bill of Rights commit the government to actively fulfilling the individual's chosen course of action for him, something in fact neither the Constitution nor the Bill of Rights does. In their seizure of the abortion issue the ideologues were doomed to bankrupt its real meaning, which is a spiritual consideration of nothing less than at what biological point one body is the ship of two souls, compared to which considerations of history and destiny are indeed piddling.

If the nature of ideology in the Twentieth Century is paradoxical, the nature of ideology in America holds its own conundrum. The large masses of Americans are not ideological: in large part they've not needed the faith in destiny that ideology offers, because America itself has come to offer its own such faith. It's hard to say how the degree of this faith might have amused or alarmed or confused the original inventors of America in all their skepticism: Washington and Franklin and Hamilton,

Samuel and John Adams, who regarded the entire endeavor of making America as a wild shot into the dark of history; even Jefferson, the most preternaturally optimistic of the lot, had his doubts and trepidations. Within a couple of generations, however, the sense of American faith had taken hold, and two hundred years later, the America born in such turmoil and passion had apparently survived the perils of that turmoil and passion in such bloody and incendiary fashion that it was shocked to feel its sense of destiny shaken after seeming to survive everything that could threaten it. The mythic affront to destiny by John Kennedy's assassination has been assessed before; it cannot be overstated, nor can the subsequent affronts of the two great assassinations that followed it five years later. By the beginning of the Reagan Era an anxiety had seeped into the soul of a country that viewed anxiety as contrary to the country's psychological temperament: Ronald Reagan renewed the American faith in its destiny in terms that were ideological. My friend in New York who told me how angry people there were with Dukakis went on to describe a dinner conversation that revolved around the Pledge of Allegiance. The conversationalists in question were moderately liberal Democrats who expressed alarm when my friend suggested he would pledge his allegiance not to the flag but to the Constitution, which of course is the same pledge George Bush or Michael Dukakis will make when one becomes president. This remark was unfathomable to the others. "The Constitution," responded one heatedly, "is only a document. The flag is a *symbol*." It's the most potent and insidious tactic of ideology to seize control of people's myths, killing the useless ones and exalting those which might be manipulated; archetypes take on a resonance that echoes in the subconscious; the symbol of America was more important to the dinner conversationalists than the authentic definition of America itself. When Michael Dukakis said in his Atlanta acceptance speech that the fall campaign would be about not ideology but competence, I remember people in the Omni Center cheering wildly. But outside the center, in the country that had come to value the physical symbols of America more than America's meaning, the statement was a rude jolt. It sounded like Dukakis was saying the campaign would not be about belief or faith, which rendered him the messenger of a secular political blasphemy. Bush made the point with devastating vividness when, upon accepting *his* nomination, he said Dukakis was a man who might make the trains run on time but had no idea where they should go.

The ideology of the Reagan Era has seized control of the imagination of the body politic as the most effective ideology does, and this will always defy analysis. Ask the public whether in the broadest sense it favors more government action in its life and it will say no; ask whether it favors that more money be spent on education or the environment or housing or health care or law enforcement and it will say yes. It does not matter, in other words, that in a matter of specific instances the public rejects the ideology of the Reagan Era: the command by the Reagan ideologues of the public's myths and archetypes and symbols, that is, the objectified components of the public's political imagination, is complete enough to win the argument. Since Dukakis himself seems quite bereft of poetry or the language of any kind of imagination, nuclear or otherwise, he's ill-equipped to make his case in such a context: only crisis and upheaval and irrevocable failure by the ideology in power will overturn that ideology, overturn the control of those archetypes and myths. Though we may point out that Dukakis has run an inept campaign, we should also consider that probably no one would have done much better in terms of the final outcome, that in fact Dukakis is a victim of a political cycle that after twenty years must still face the consequences of its time in power before it can be closed full circle. Dukakis as well carries, fairly or not, the baggage of Democratic liberal failure. Conservative commentators are incensed that Dukakis is unwilling to accept the mantle

of liberalism as they've defined it, and argue that this unwilling-
ness is philosophical deceit. My own guess is that the accusations
of liberalism are genuinely baffling to Dukakis. Though his social
priorities are liberal for the most part, his persona is unmistakably
that of a conservative who would be nothing but sternly disap-
proving of the hedonistic excesses of the last twenty years. His
fiscal instincts are conservative as well, as is his stubborn refusal
to make extravagant promises to the various interest groups to
whom liberal candidates usually make such promises. Dukakis
probably remembers, ironically and bitterly, how he enraged
Massachusetts liberals in his first term as governor, and thus lost
his first bid for reelection, by savagely slashing social programs in
order to bring to the state's finances the conservative virtues of
order and accountability; he's also probably chagrined at how he's
never been really regarded by liberal activists as one of theirs,
most of them having thrown their lot to Jesse Jackson and Paul
Simon in the primaries and caucuses. Thus he inherits the
enmity of conservatives who believe he's too liberal and the
indifference of liberals who believe he's not particularly liberal at
all. Gary Hart wanted to be the first major postideological
candidate of postideological America, assessing as he did that
Ronald Reagan was the apotheosis of ideological America, the
most and also the last ideological president, and that Reagan's
departure would signal a change in the way people deliberated
the truth in both its grand and banal forms. What Hart didn't
figure was that the psychology of a people wouldn't change as
easily as their reasoning; and if Hart didn't figure this it goes
without saying that Dukakis wouldn't either, so far removed is he
from a cosmic sense of things. The real dichotomy of ideology
under Reagan reduced all the components of the political
imagination to a childlike choice, between an America portrayed
by Reagan as always right, and an America portrayed by the Left
as always wrong. It doesn't take a genius to figure out which
would be the more attractive. Yet this has eluded the American

Left, or else only underscored its hatefulness; and its spokesmen—counterculture columnists and Stalinist apologists still trying to tell us it was really the United States that shot down that Korean airplane six years ago—have been enormously invaluable in framing this choice for Reagan, as they were invaluable in sabotaging Jimmy Carter from the first eighteen months of his presidency until his reelection. I know, because I voted for John Anderson in 1980, which makes me the biggest jerk of all, except of course for you jerks who voted for Barry Commoner. Now I understand that it's probably in the longrange interest of the United States, assuming it's going to survive long range, to vote for George Bush, because when Americans wake up from the Reagan dream, it's fitting that Bush's face be the one that greets them with the bad news.

Cynic then: surely I'm cynical enough to rejoice in the logic of this with a vote for Bush, surely if my pending audit by Michael Dukakis is not enough to push me into the ranks of the Grand Old Party, my cynicism will. Dukakis' campaign has been a Buster Keaton movie ever since Atlanta, with whole swaths of the calendar squandered in Boston, with whole regiments of the Democratic Party left waiting for the call to arms, with strategies that shift every twenty-four hours, appearing to be about one thing one day and something entirely different the next. That these people behind Dukakis, and the candidate himself, nursed the hubris to suppose the election was a fait accompli fairly raises a plethora of suspicions about the manner in which they might bungle the operation of government. Dukakis' ideas for resolving the country's budget crisis are artificial; he has a host of legitimate complaints about the country's welfare without convincing specifics as to how they'll be resolved, and though he often speaks of the country's need for an international vision, in eighteen months he has yet to offer one, a failure which only emphasizes his total lack of foreign-policy experience. His concentration on a newly revitalized conventional military force in Europe is all right in itself, but the implication that it will reduce defense expenditures is as false as his tax-collection crusade for erasing the deficit. Several ideas having to do with college-tuition and home-financing programs are good but nonetheless lack a schematic in much the way his foreign-policy proposals do; and their formlessness is only enhanced by his bloodless presentation of them. In the first televised presidential debate in September, people in the audience actually laugh at Dukakis when he claims to be tough on crime; in the second debate in October, he's apparently unfazed by an attempt to put the question in personal terms, a snuff-movie of a question having to do with his wife's hypothetical rape and murder. These responses are all the more baffling because the facts of the matter are not unfavorable to Dukakis: the prison furlough program in Massachusetts, from which one convicted murderer escaped to commit mayhem in another state—an issue on which Dukakis has taken enormous heat—was in fact begun not by Dukakis but rather by a Republican predecessor; it is not particularly dissimilar from some forty other such programs in the country; crime in Massachusetts under Dukakis has gone not up but down. Dukakis seems to regard this issue, and its defense, as beneath him. Given that it would take a certain amount of shamelessness to recount personal tragedy in his expressed concern about crime (his father was once beaten and robbed, his brother the victim of hit-and-run manslaughter), and given that he is obviously un-comfortable offering such an account, it would not on the other hand be so manipulative to make the case that while he might in any such situation feel the hunger for vengeance, vengeance is not the tenor of a civilized society. The public may not agree with this argument but they might respect it more than his responses which are stunning for the way they're empty of passion. One wishes that Dukakis resorted to following his political instincts in such matters but at this point it's questionable whether his political instincts are any good, an unsettling doubt about a candidate who's also unwilling to trust emotional communication. Should he be elected, one fears he's bound to disappoint people, and the consequences of that failure may be worse than his failure to win the job in the first place.

Thus, the case for rejecting Dukakis and embracing the Republican alternative might be a formidable one; and none of it is here or there. Because the Republican alternative is in particular George Bush. Have I made my feelings entirely clear about George Bush? I'd hate to think I've been obscure in the matter of George Bush, I couldn't be happy if there's uncertainty in this regard. It may say everything about George Bush that, since there are many moments in the first debate when he's simply incoherent, it's thus regarded as monumental success in the second debate when he constructs whole sentences with beginnings, middles and ends, an intellectual evolution which a wildly grateful nation celebrates by promptly declaring the election over. If by some chance this does not say everything about Bush, let us point out that if Dukakis' domestic ideas are unformed, Bush doesn't appear to have any; that asked which of a dozen colossal weapons systems proposed by the Reagan administration the country can't afford, he names ones that no longer exist; that nothing more irresponsible has been proposed in this campaign than Bush's promise to raise taxes under no circumstances whatsoever, unless one were to count the way he attaches to this promise he-man imitations of fortitude ("Read my lips"), thus obligating himself to govern as either a fraud or a fool who must keep such a promise even when the economic disaster of the future dictates otherwise. On the issue of abortion, and Bush's opposition to it, his reply in the first debate ("I haven't sorted out the penalties") demonstrates to whatever extent one still needs to have it demonstrated the man's casual lack of interest in remote situations that have nothing to do with him personally and may not have a political payoff; Bush hasn't sorted out the penalties because he'll never be pregnant. Why sort out the penalties on an issue on which you've changed your position four times in the last eight years? Why sort out the penalties at all when a whole new position on the issue may, two or six or twelve months hence, be more politically expedient? Bush's positions on one matter or another can be unearthed only in the polling data of his campaign's computers; on the wall of the war room at Republican headquarters is a map of the Bush Conscience, with little flags reading "Bush once stood here" dotting the sovereign nation of Abortion, the small island empire of Supply-Side Economics. For weeks now Bush has traveled in a plastic information bubble where nothing of the outside world gets to him and nothing of him gets to the outside world except a gesture glimpsed through the plastic, his nonexistent immune system protected from the infections of an unsupervised unpredicted confrontation with a toxic question, to which he might have to supply an answer that someone else hasn't already supplied to him. Of course in their debates both candidates are rehearsed to the gills; you can see Dukakis practicing his summations in the bathroom mirror while he shaves over and over the heaviest political beard since Nixon's. Nonetheless one still senses that the words coming out of Dukakis are things that are of him; his conscientious intelligence is manifest and apparently capable of functioning independent of a TelePrompTer. When Dukakis remembers, he remembers what he knows. Bush never remembers what he knows. Bush remembers what he remembers. It's true that Dukakis seems to have trouble remembering what he feels, and it's in contrast to this that Bush seems more agreeable; over a drink, he may well be. He might walk into my motel room this very moment and, in a trivial sort of way, I'd like him. It's indicative of grace in Bush that at one moment during the second debate when his own partisans begin to boo a Dukakis answer, Bush actually raises his hand to quiet them; it's this kind of instinctive generosity the public has sensed about him and seized on. Even the impulse behind some of the malicious things Bush has said and done doesn't seem personally malicious in itself; but there's malice nonetheless in the naive act that has malicious consequences, and Bush hasn't really seemed so naive as he's conducted the most dishonest and venal campaign by a major presidential nominee in a generation. It's a campaign that has truly hurt the country, first in the way it's encouraged Americans to paint a particularly nasty and selfcentered and ignorant selfportrait, and second in the way it's offered no configuration of a future, which means that when Bush is elected, he'll have been elected to do nothing at all. Bush's sense of obligation to his country is too mediocre to take this into account. He's a man who over the years has been picked for job after job by president after president for one consistent reason, as revealed recently in the released transcripts of the Nixon White House, where Bush held a number of ambassadorial positions as well as the chairmanship of the Republican National Committee; and that reason was not his intelligence or integrity or insight or wisdom or honesty or strength or experience or any sense of commitment to any conviction. That reason has always been loyalty, a loyalty which chose to be naive too often to assume the innocence of true naïveté, a loyalty which never manifested itself in a single serious decision until the moment it decided to make Dan Quayle vice president of the United States. What the establishment has always loved about Bush is his amiable amorality, how you can drop a moral principle into the well of him and wait an infinity to hear the splash at the bottom.

Bloody earring in the palm of my hand. In the night, in my motel, I think it tries to speak to me. I think it's saying maybe I'm not going to be a Republican this year after all. Maybe it's just a failure of nerve on my part, let's put it down to that. Ventura mutters in his sleep of the Devil, which isn't to suggest he doesn't know what he's saying; he speaks of the Devil even in waking moments. "Remember," he says in the dark, "how two months ago Bush went on that fishing trip with James Baker? He vanished for a week? And when he came back, he was an *entirely different person?"* George Bush, in other words, may be the Robert Johnson of American politics. He vanished with his guitar in the feeble fingers that weren't good enough to play it, vanished into thin air and then came back an entirely different person, though with the same guitar. This may be, in other words, the biggest mischief by the Devil since, if not Robert Johnson, then at least Jimi Hendrix's dying only days before he was to record with Miles Davis. "The Devil did that too," Ventura explains knowingly; the Devil was not going to let a union like that happen. George and Dan are right up the Devil's alley, but Jimi and Miles were too delirious and scary even for the Devil. The next thing I know, Ventura's asleep, I hear him. The next thing I know, it seems hours but the clock says only twenty minutes, I hear her knocking on the door of my room. She comes to me having rejected my secrets but having listened in on my dream; she knows that either I've abandoned the new United States or they've abandoned me. I sit up suddenly. I grab my coat in the dark and shove the earring into my pocket to hide it. I put the coat back where it was, on a chair near the bathroom. Ventura slumbers on. I listen to her at the door; we'll vanish for a week and come back entirely different people. I sit on the bed the rest of the night listening to her at the door, until the knocking stops at dawn.

• • •

It may only be a cosmic accident that human technology and imagination developed to the point of ushering in the nuclear age and the television age at the same time. Nonetheless the two in tandem had the effect of transforming human memory, since memories are the psychic increments of time; in the face of an abyss that blew the hands off our clocks and set our compasses spinning wildly, where all experience is rendered by television technologically communal, memory becomes first literalized, then reduced to vivid moments not necessarily threaded to anything else. These moments break loose of the gravity of history, which means that history, even as my generation understood it in our youth, is reduced to surrealism, defiant of rational chronology; children today believe Watergate took place in the early part of the Twentieth Century, and that the Civil War took place in an entirely different century from the Nineteenth, assuming children know what Watergate and the Civil War are at all. That this is a failure of the educational system does not rebut the underlying sense of Americans that history is absurd and without value; educational failure conforms to the way technology and imagination contradict each other, having developed polar truths. Memories may be called up to our consciousness now like bits of information called up on a computer; when memories are this easily shuffled in time, they're subject to change and control. In the process they're politicized as never before.

A brilliant Republican commercial on the airwaves now shows grim and distressing images of the Seventies, to the voice of someone crooning "I Remember You." The you in this case is the beleaguered image of Jimmy Carter. This fifteen or twenty seconds conceptualizes our memory of Carter; there's no doubt in our minds what we remember of him, people hanging their heads while they wait on the hoods of their cars in lines for gasoline. The truth, we might only incidentally mention, is that gas lines began, and were at their worst, not during the presidency of Jimmy Carter, but during the presidency of Gerald Ford. But memory, in conjunction with people's myths, has been altered to something different; and television literalizes the remembered reality and the mythic reality as it has come to literalize a thousand more trivial realities. Ronald Reagan was the embodiment of this; he literalized his own heroism, as a man who before his assassination had never done anything truly heroic but play heroes, and was finally hired to play our hero on the grandest public scale.

An odd thing is happening now, three weeks before the election. The date on the calendar says 17 October, but the election is already over, the eighth of November has come and gone. George Bush has already been elected, we already remember him elected; we're already living the aftermath of the election, three weeks before it's happened. The election won't even be the aftermath of itself, it will rather be the aftermath of the aftermath. Last week, in an extraordinary half hour, the television news program "Nightline" spent an entire show on a poll it had taken. The footage that accompanied the poll offered the usual token caveats and equivocations, but the election was discussed in what was indisputably the past tense. Michael Dukakis' candidacy was discussed in the past tense; there was much analysis about why he had lost the election, three weeks before the election had happened. This memory of Dukakis' defeat established a context for, and was reinforced by, the second presidential debate which took place the following night: the moment Dukakis walked onstage in Los Angeles, we remembered him as the man who once lost a presidential election that hadn't happened yet.

My friends on both the Right and Left make the same contention about the media, which is that it is biased against them. My friends on the Left argue that the press is the organ of the corporate-political establishment, despite its role in ending the Vietnam War and initiating the revelations of the Watergate scandal. My friends on the Right bemoan the liberal brainwashing of the public despite the public's inclination to elect conservative Republicans four times in the last five elections, with the fifth in six now at hand. Some massive tilt in the earth on Election Day 1972 or 1984 apparently sent millions of McGovern-chanting or Mondale-intoning liberal zombies tumbling onto the Nixon and Reagan levers in the ballot booths. The fact is that at one time or another my friends on both the Right and Left have been correct, and it doesn't matter. The fact is that the press doesn't really have the courage of its convictions even if it has any, and this has become more characteristic of the media over the years rather than less, though it can be traced back to the genesis of television news, its proud selfcongratulatory exposés of Joseph McCarthy having come years after most of the damage was already done. The irony is that Ronald Reagan's success was bought largely at the price of Richard Nixon's failure, as far as press coverage was concerned. Intimidated after Vietnam and Watergate by charges of liberal bias, the press determined it could cut Jimmy Carter very little slack; and television journalism in particular gave Reagan a free ride for five years, beginning with all his outlandish promises in 1980 about balancing budgets and cutting taxes and launching lavish military buildups at the same time. The press knew this was either dishonest or deranged, but more than that it knew a winner when it saw one, and a loser when it saw one, and which Reagan was, and which Carter. The press felt it only fair, and perhaps significant to its public esteem, to despise a haggard and bumbling man of Carter's honesty and good intentions as much as a shrewd and skillful man of Nixon's selfinterested corruption. Three years into Reagan's presidency, major newsmagazines were only beginning to nervously relate the more striking examples of the commander-in-chief's blithe interest in matters some might find pertinent: lowly congressmen gingerly explaining to the president the triad nature of our defense system, and how it differs from that of the Soviets. These reports were usually couched in larger vantage points constructed in ways to make certain the public wouldn't hate the press for telling it the truth. By the time Reagan, in his first debate with Walter Mondale in 1984, revealed to the world that for four years he'd believed nuclear missiles could be called back after they'd been launched, the public didn't even blink. When Reagan, as the messiah of disembodied historical memory, said that Hitler's SS were just ordinary young German soldiers, the public was rather more shaken, but only for a week. Reagan, as has been noted often enough for it to become part of his whimsical legend, also remembers touring the concentration camps immediately after World War Two, when in fact he never left Hollywood. Gary Hart, on the other hand, changed the way he signed his name, and the press pronounced him crackers.

By a similar irony, George Bush's success with the press was bought in part at the price of Gary Hart's failure. The public was of two minds about the Hart scandal that drove him from the presidential race, and these conclusions were not necessarily contradictory. The first was that Hart shouldn't be president. The second was that the press had gone too far in helping the public make this determination. When, in a television interview with Bush earlier in the year, Dan Rather displayed an unseemly aggression, it triggered in the public the memory of that second conclusion; afterward the press backed off Bush almost entirely, dealing only with the technical conduct of his campaign and leaving aside questions about Bush's involvement in some of the rather less polished aspects of Ronald Reagan's eight-year adventure in public relations. Reagan at least ran on a program, specious as it was; Bush has run further on nothing than any modern presidential candidate in history, exceeding even the rather ethereal candidacies of Reagan '84 (who ran on the record of his first term), Carter '76 (who ran against the record of the two presidents before him) and Nixon '68 (who ran against the disintegrating state of the Union). Questions entirely relevant to Bush '88, that is his performance as vice president, apparently just rub people the wrong way. The press, frustrated by its talent for being manipulated, channeled that frustration into the Dan Quayle story when Quayle was nominated for vice president, only to be manipulated even more. Rather than subject Quayle's candidacy to questions about its political fitness, the press instead asked not whether the candidate slept with a blond lobbyist eight years ago, since no one suggested he did, but whether he *wanted* to sleep with her. Even Dan Quayle didn't deserve this. The public rightly reacted against this kind of interrogation; Gary Hart had already died for these sins. Thus there remains over the course of the campaign public resentment about the way the press has covered Quayle, and the press knows it; and particularly after the television debate early this month between Quayle and Lloyd Bentsen, the Republicans have used it. Quayle has become a victim. Having called Michael Dukakis crazy, unpatriotic, the benefactor of murderers and rapists, the supporter of child pornographers, and the husband of a flag burner, one Republican politician after another, in the manner of every bully who's really a crybaby at heart, sobbed with indignation when Bentsen told Quayle he was not Jack Kennedy. "Now you leave poor Danny Quayle alone," Minnesota Senator Rudy Boschwitz blubbered to Sam Donaldson on the air, "you've had your fun." The president himself somberly called Bentsen's comment a cheap shot, presumably to be distinguished from another cheap shot, now ancient history, when the president called Dukakis an invalid. Of course that was only a joke, for which the president later said he *thought* he was sorry. At any rate, within hours the press was indeed leaving Danny Quayle alone, having had its fun. The public relief was palpable.

In this same atmosphere the press has labored mightily to be unscrupulously evenhanded. Unscrupulous because the evenhandedness has defeated the truth, and sabotaged the press's function to report the truth even as it may have indulged the press's role as electoral referee. By now the air is filled with stories about the negative nature of the campaign, and the extent to which the public's fed up with it. In September Ted Koppel, who usually deserves his reputation as the smartest and fairest of the television interviewers, did a program on the Pledge of Allegiance which implied that the demagoguery on the issue was equally divided between the two campaigns. As the target of this particular hit-and-run, Dukakis is apparently to be held accountable for obstructing traffic and, when the car backs up over him several times for good measure, making a mess in the street as well. In the same fashion, one news commentator after another is careful to identify the campaign as being negative "on both sides," and when Bush is belatedly condemned for his questioning of Dukakis' patriotism, Dukakis is hurriedly taken to task in the same breath for labeling the tactic McCarthyism. How precisely must a situation present itself before one can gingerly apply the term, if one cannot apply it here? "What *bothers* him so much about the Pledge of Allegiance?" is the way Bush has most famously put it. This isn't to say Dukakis hasn't been out of order. His threat that Republicans would begin chomping up Social Security cards is a careless leap of logic at best and an unsubstantiated scare tactic at worst, and that's ignoring the hard fact that a freeze in Social Security payments may be as necessarily inevitable as both a tax raise and a defense cut, no matter who is president. It was also a nasty bit of character assassination for Dukakis, in the second debate, to throw in Robert Bork's name when talking about the crooks of the Reagan administration; whatever one thinks of Bork's politics, his personal honesty has not been at issue. Liberals so incensed about the dishonest savaging of Dukakis' record did not mind distorting Bork's on a number of subjects during his Supreme Court hearings. Yet in the end Dukakis' transgressions are pigeon droppings on the cow pie known as the Bush campaign, however much the press may proliferate rationalizations to the contrary. Is its sense of proportion so bankrupt that it sees no difference between mocking a candidate as born with a silver foot in his mouth, and insinuating a candidate may be mentally unstable and latently un-American? Having implied or suggested outright that Dukakis' campaign is as scurrilous as Bush's, the press than identifies the ineptitude of Dukakis' response to Bush's charges; the unveiled hint is that, for that ineptitude, Dukakis deserves to be lied about and the public deserves to be lied to. Finally, the press serves as accomplice. No visual images of the Reagan-Bush record on toxic wastes and acid rain and wilderness ravishment and clean water vetoes and the neutering of the Environmental Protection Agency are ever juxtaposed against that of George Bush standing on the docks of Boston Harbor, and thus those thirty seconds become the operable public memory which erases a seven-year reality, a memory to be called up to the public consciousness again and again. Perhaps the networks regarded it as incumbent on the Dukakis campaign to provide such a juxtaposition. If so, then the television media has reduced itself to being the traffic cops of our manipulated memories, negotiating jammed intersections where the order of red and green lights is foolish in the context of a vicious rush hour.

Throughout the year as the currents of change and continuity have run alongside each other, sometimes converging and other times forking, one seeming to rush stronger and faster than the other, then the other stronger and faster, the failure of both Dukakis and Bush has not been in acting as agents for their particular currents, but in understanding and speaking to the other current that was sometimes converging with their own. No one misunderstands that Dukakis is the candidate of change and that Bush is the candidate of continuity; what is confounding for so many is that even those who feel the need for change want the continuity of some things, and even those who feel the need for continuity want some other things changed. People accept the way their candidates speak to their primary concern but are unnerved by the way the candidates fail to speak to the secondary concern. In a summer of apocalyptic images, images of fire and disintegration, the concern for change was primary; when autumn came and people could finally take some refuge from those images, they fled to the shores of continuity. In the same way that the election is phenomenal for the way its own aftermath has preceded it, one notices a nostalgia for Ronald Reagan before he's even gone. We celebrate these things before they happen and the celebration is dispirited, puny in its noise and dance. The people can decry the meanness and emptiness of the campaign, but the truth is we're up to our necks in our own responsibility for it; we endorse the commercials and slurs by our own compliance with the sentiments they express. On television, which in the last two weeks of the campaign is almost wholly obsessed with covering its own coverage of the campaign, people are interviewed in the street expressing dismay about the campaign. Asked which candidate they prefer and why, however, they then parrot some piece of misinformation they saw in a TV ad, as well as punishing candidates like Robert Dole or Bruce Babbitt who conveyed some unpleasant truth. In an election in which more people were involved in the nomination process than ever before, over a vertiginous schedule of primaries and caucuses, Bush and Dukakis emerged as the nominees because they embodied what the people wanted, just as Nixon, Carter and Reagan did, however much we may disavow them later. Complaints about the choice between Bush and Dukakis are dishonest and more often than not expressed by people who didn't give a moment's concern to the process as it unfolded over eight months; suddenly they wonder loudly and bitterly about the prospects presented to them. Now there's a rush to be a part of the memory of the choice. The polls are on us like locusts, and the news for Michael Dukakis is nightmarish. Seventeen points ahead in the summer of apocalyptic images, he is now seventeen points behind; even given the acknowledged chaos of his campaign and his own flaws as a candidate, a thirty-four-point shift is beyond the pale of political rationality. Dukakis could have announced a past history of cannibalism or sexual escapades with Dobermans and it would not have accounted for thirty-four points. Something is taking hold here; the zeitgeist of the autumn has become the reference point for the choice, and has infiltrated its components. When Dukakis won his first debate with Bush, and Bentsen the second with Quayle, public sentiment didn't so much as ripple; Bush won the third and the dam broke. There's almost a collective understanding that though the Democrats might be smarter or better-informed on the issues, the current of continuity has its own power, and now through the end of October it sweeps public memory on its voyage into the storm. All that remains to be answered is the question of Bush's own nostalgia, how soon we'll begin to miss him before he's stayed too long or has even yet arrived. Even more interesting may be our nostalgia for Dukakis, who's already becoming humanized by his pending humiliation. "What's the difference between George Bush and me?" he asks an audience rhetorically today in Kalamazoo, Michigan; and someone in the crowd shouts an unexpected answer: "You're real and he's not." Dukakis is visibly amazed and uplifted by this faceless response. But nostalgia by its very nature renders our memories unreal, which is why we so value it. How will it render our memories of men who seemed unreal to begin with. . . .

• • •

But I sense something around the next bend. I wake to the moment of the road, but lie on the backseat half an hour feeling the road and thinking. After a while we come somewhere to eat, the sun is already overhead. The restaurant is in back of a store; we eat silently. The driver is reading a newspaper; the passenger watches out the restaurant window. I sense something. I think they do too. The passenger hides from me something, all his black secrets. The waitress takes away the plates and the man who drives unfolds a map on the table. He runs his finger along a barely marked road, he runs his finger around each bend. I sense something today.

Across the north of Arizona no one says much. Ventura's taking me somewhere to show me something; we wind our way through the Indian mesas as the afternoon flees from our faces. There's a story on the radio that one out of every three Americans does not understand that the earth revolves around the sun. More than half of Americans do not know that light travels faster than sound. Sally is in the backseat, where she can always keep an eye on the both of us. "The savings and loans are all in debt now," Ventura's saying. "The corporations are in debt. The farms are all in debt. The consumers are all in debt. The government's in debt. Nothing in the country is solvent. When they all collapse, what will hold things up? America's like a girl you loved in school. You grow up and you leave school and she becomes a whore and gets all these diseases and you still love her. You'll never not love her." We come to a fork in the road and he's remembering which way to go. He has some place in mind that we're going to now; some part of me that doesn't understand why only knows I don't want to see it. Some part of me that doesn't understand why knows that it's part of the destiny of this day that I will see it: I turn, suddenly, for no reason at all, to look at Sally. She looks back for a long minute and then away, out the window. Ventura's warmed up now. "When you think about it, there's something to be said for the junkie," he explains. "A junkie," he explains, "has only *one* problem. He doesn't have any other problems. He wakes up in the morning and there's only one thing he has to do that day. His life is simple. Why couldn't we be junkies? Our lives would be simple. We'd have one thing to do when we woke up in the morning. But no, we couldn't have been something as easy as junkies, we had to be Americans." Now the country has opened up. We've emerged from the shadows of a ravine into a canyon endless and flat enough to swallow up the rest of the day or the rest of the week. It's red and starched with a white light that weaves into the minutes and miles. The mesa of our destination is before us.

We're there now.

The mesa rises senselessly monolithic from the crater floor. We cross the flat plain to the base of the mesa and Ventura finds the road up. The road is only a narrow strip of dirt that coils up the side of the mesa; it leaves no room for error as we drive it. I have no idea how high the mesa is but it towers above the endless open canyon. It takes us about ten minutes to get to the top; none of us says anything. We're alone in our ascent; right now everything for as far as we can see seems empty.

At the top of the mesa is a small village, what turns out to be the new part of the village. Here there are a few other cars parked beside the buildings; there's a tourist office that closed an hour ago. It's now a little before six in the afternoon. The sun is still well above the horizon. We bring the car to a stop in front of the tourist office, a large dog runs up to greet the door. Only occasionally is someone to be seen in the distance other than children riding their bikes in the dust of the mesa's top. Everyone in this village is an Indian; a startlingly beautiful small Indian girl circles us on her bicycle in curiosity. Ventura gets out of the car, but for a while I sit where I am, and Sally doesn't move either. I think I'm fixed to where I am mostly by the way Sally isn't moving. That's when I know.

It's Leap Day.

Then I hear her and out of the corner of my eye I see her open the door on the driver's side. I get out too and all three of us stand there in the dust together, in the shadow of the closed tourist office. The little Indian girl keeps circling us on her bike.

A sheriff's car drives up. An Indian wearing a uniform politely asks if he can help us, which means he's wondering what we're doing here. Ventura tells him we're just looking around and the officer nods and explains that the tourist office is closed. We can remain in the new village if we want but the old village, several hundred feet away at the end of the mesa top, is closed to anyone without a tourist guide. Ventura nods silently at this. I feel we're violating something here. The sheriff drives off and we begin to walk through the village; the little girl follows along. Sally smiles at her and says hello, and the little girl asks if we want to buy some souvenirs. She asks if we want to buy dishes or a shirt. She can take us to her mother's house now if we want. We shake our heads sadly, but she's not disappointed because she doesn't really accept our answers. She keeps following us on her bike; the dog trails along behind us too. Why don't you want to buy a shirt, the little girl wants to know. I walk to the edge of the village, to the edge of the mesa beyond the edge of the village. At the edge of the mesa the red beneath my feet gives way to the white of gaping space, and the blue of the sky beyond the edge of the gaping space. The earth soars up silently into my eyes. It's far away. It's a distant planet where we were half an hour ago, it's far below us; the village is as rooted to the sky by its ceilings as it is to the mesa below us, the mesa itself is more of the sky than of the earth. It's caught in a web of clear temporal arteries that clutch the mesa to the heart of space above it. I turn from one side to the next to see the planet whirling beneath me. Not far from me are other Indians who live in the village; they are casual in their wonder of the vision before them. The wonder of it is for them only the banal stuff of days. I turn to Ventura and Sally behind me; to my shock they don't seem interested. "It's unbelievable," I explain simply, dully. Ventura nods but says, "This isn't what I want to show you." Sally is already looking in the direction of what Ventura wants to show me.

He's here. After all this time, after a hundred and sixty-two years he's here. Now that he's to be found I wonder if I want to find him.

Ventura's now walking to the other side of the village. I leave the edge of the mesa and follow him, Sally follows him, though she knows where she's going without either of us. We come to the end of the new village where the mesa begins to run out, narrowing to a thread of itself and leading to a smaller part on the other side of a stone bridge. There on the other side is the ancient village of Walpi. It is by legend, and perhaps by history, the oldest inhabited city in the Western Hemisphere. Some date it eight hundred to a thousand years old, eight hundred to a thousand years in which people have lived in it. It seems to rise out of the mesa itself, pocked with black doors and black windows. Looking at it one can hardly imagine stepping amidst it even with a tourist guide; it's the arrogance of a modern Western mind such as mine to believe that the treading of my footsteps would send the village and the mesa below it raining down to the planet in rubble. As though it's so old it could not stand a modern footstep, even though on the face of its age such a footstep is but the snap of two fingers in infinity. We stand watching it without remark.

Suddenly, in the black doorway that faces us from across the thread of the mesa, there steps an old man. He is tall, his skin pale; he doesn't wave but only watches us in return. After a moment Sally silently approaches the bridge and crosses, untouched by the rules of tourists.

I cross the bridge slowly, waiting for him to wave to me. When I'm near him I can see it's too much for him to wave, to raise his hand to me, I see it's everything he has for him to stand in the doorway of the ancient village. He begins to totter as I'm ten feet from him; he buckles and I rush to catch him.

In the dark of the room behind him an old Indian woman also rushes to him. The two of us look quickly at each other, we hold him up and help him to the blankets that lie in the corner of the dark room. A candle burns there. We lay him on the blanket. She goes to get him something to drink. The whole time he doesn't look at me at all, he stares ahead of him breathing deeply. He knows I'm here though, he knows it's me. But I might as well have left him only yesterday, it might as well have been only a week ago we were in Virginia together. The Indian woman comes back and gives him some water while I wipe his head with a rag. When he closes his eyes to sleep, she stands again without looking at me and disappears into the dark of the room. It may be there's a passage there in the dark or there's nothing but the dark. I lean back against the wall, afraid to be close to him, angry at him I guess. I guess I am. In a moment he's sleeping.

They told me you were dead and I knew they were liars. They told me you were alive and I silenced them with my knife.

When I open my eyes it's dark beyond the door. It's night. I rise and stand in the door and look out over the valley below the mesa. Not a light shines in its basin. Across the stone bridge the driver and his passenger are gone. I go back into the room and sit with him.

I will tell you this dream I had just now, I say to him; there's no sound to his sleep now. He may be asleep or he may be awake listening to me. Here's this dream. It's about a thing you made, it was a country. We had come back from Paris, but instead of coming to live here with the Indians we stayed together in a house and you made a country and ruled it in rags. We were the scandal of the nation. You owned me and I loved you, and then they told me one night you died. I went looking for you. I searched the country you made for you, but they'd forgotten you. They told me you were dead and I knew they were liars, they told me you were alive and I silenced them with my knife. I left no witnesses behind me. The country you made changed to a different country the longer I went. I got a ride with two men; they were fools. They were too foolish to wonder if you were alive, they were too foolish to believe you were dead. We crossed territory together until the country behind us was only a memory.

It wasn't much of a dream actually, but when I woke just a moment ago it was as though I hadn't seen you in a hundred and sixty-two years. When I woke just a moment ago I stood up and went to the door and looked across the bridge believing for a moment I'd see two men there. Like most dreams though it passes now from memory, and I barely remember the men at all.

Are you awake?

The days pass in Walpi. I see now you were waiting for me to wake up so you could go. It startles me, some days later, when you suddenly grasp my hand. It feels like a hundred and sixty-two years since you touched me. I grasp your hand back. Do you have to go? Can't we spend more time together first? I finally bring myself to lie down against you, I finally bring myself to put my head on your old chest. I listen to the sound in you of your heart gasping for just another moment. Something else feels different about it, different from the way I used to lay my head on your chest; I reach to my ear to feel its lobe, naked and torn. Once I wore something there and it's gone, something you gave me.

Do you have to go?

The days pass. You clutch at me when I want to pull away, when I can't stand to hear the desperate heart in you. There are no more dreams when I sleep. The last dream is gone utterly, the last tatter of it blown to an unseen distance. The country of the dream goes with it, I guess.

You clutch at me when I want to be alone.

The man who made the country of the dream goes with it, I guess.

And one night I just wake and you're not there anymore. The blankets are empty; there isn't the sound in the dark of another soul. I think I should get up and look for you. Thomas? my brain says, but not my mouth. I keep your name to myself. I lie there in the blankets in case you should come back, but I know you're not coming back. I wonder if in the daylight I'll find some trace of you, some husk of you, the innards of which have dribbled away. But I know there won't even be that. I lie in the blankets. I was the president's whore, I'm a liar if I pretend I feel no honor in it. I lie in the blankets and after an hour has passed, and then another, and then another, at the hour before daylight when he has not come back, I decide I'll pretend to be asleep in the way I used to do when he came to me sometimes. I'll pretend not so as to fool him, since there's no more fooling him; I'm not sure who I'm fooling, who I'm pretending for. It may be myself.

And as the hour before daylight has almost passed, in the last moment before daylight when I believe I've finally fooled them all, I have a vision:

• • •

This morning Josef cuts the tree. I wake to the sound of his saw beneath our window. The tree in the front yard has been leaning for years now over the driveway, and one can see where the roots of it have grown so long and large beneath our apartment that the foundation is beginning to rip. An ominous crack runs along the base of the building. The assault on the tree by Josef and his saw is fierce, slashing. He takes off the top, then takes off the middle, then returns some hours from now to dig up the trunk. One of our cats is fond of this tree; it's his sanctuary from other cats and a terrible world. The only reason he goes out of the apartment at all is to go up the tree, from where he can see much of the city, the way I see much of it from our upstairs window. This morning Slim darts from the apartment and makes for the tree; but the tree isn't there. Accidentally he runs up the wrong tree; he knows it's wrong. He's a befuddled little animal today. There's no explaining to him that the tree had to go to preserve the foundation of the apartment.

When Ventura and I drove up a few weeks ago and I pulled my pack from beneath the voodoo candles in the trunk, and walked in the door of our apartment, the look on Astrid's face revealed to me a suspicion that I would in fact not return at all. It also revealed a suspicion that I looked rather out of place here now, and that there would be a period of time when she'd have to accommodate my presence and reconcile it to her own year just past. All the electricity of the year, in the meantime, has emptied out across the Southwest; I can take hold of anything and not have to worry about feeling something. The currents have come to a stop and then dried up altogether, and things are dark from the missing blue light of their spark.

My father has had an extraordinary autumn. After his double bypass he returned home to get weaker and weaker; the doctors put him back in the hospital where they discovered he had an ulcer and was bleeding to nothing. They treated the ulcer and he returned home to get weaker and weaker; the doctors examined him and decided he had pneumonia; in the course of trying to determine the source of the pneumonia they found on an X ray a shadow over his lung. Two weeks later they removed a tumor. He returned home after several more weeks in the hospital to find he could not walk, at which point the doctors examined him to find a clot in his leg. They have inserted a filter at the top of his leg to prevent the clot from rising in his body, and are thinning the blood to the degree the ulcer will allow. It's mortifying to my dad for everything to break down this way, all at once. The doctors have found no other trace of the cancer in him. He's resolved to get well and frets over the time it takes him. He's giving his body deadlines to meet, and categorizes the days as up days and down days.

Last weekend was my twenty-year high school reunion. I considered this event with all the dread any normally psychotic person should feel about it. It was held in a hotel not five minutes from where I live, so logistics provided no excuse for not going. Nonetheless I had decided against going and almost got away with it when the phone rang a little before eleven o'clock. It was two guys from school wondering where I was; so I got dressed and went. I approached the ballroom with trepidation and was discovered immediately. I had chatty interactions with people I hadn't seen in twenty years. None of them of course was who he or she really was. They were caught in bodies and personalities that weren't theirs; sometimes in the middle of a conversation I had a fleeting glimpse of what they really looked like inside what they looked like, who they really were inside who they were. Sometimes I had a fleeting glimpse of the kernel of the person; it was as though I were talking to a relative of the person I once knew, or some stranger who had once been quite good friends with the person I once knew. I tiptoed around the room wondering who I was going to bump into that bore a vague resemblance to someone I should remember. I saw the girl I went with as a senior; luckily, she was the most familiar in many ways, we talked rather easily after not having seen each other for so long, after having gone on to love other people or bear their children. I left when two hours had passed. It's not too soon to worry about the next such affair ten years from now.

I went to see *Bird*, Clint Eastwood's movie about Charlie Parker. It's a fine movie, even a brilliant one, infused with moral truth and shorn of moral preciousness, and told in bebop time. The life of race in the movie, the blackness of the movie, is without selfconsciousness or timidity. It's good that a conservative Republican was the one who had soul and vision and courage to make such a movie; only narrower minds will be surprised. The other night at home I was taping Francis Coppola's *Godfather Saga* on television. It was a frustrating experience, trying to tape around the news bulletins. There were news bulletins all night; I got the distinct impression an election was taking place somewhere, not that far from here. Was there an election this year? In a country where men are the incarnations of memory, I've been having these lapses. I forget things. I forget myself. A few nights later there was only one bulletin. John Mitchell died. John Mitchell was an attorney general of the United States once. Hired, rather in the fashion of another recent attorney general, to render justice a nauseating joke; another of these guys who claims to so love his country he wouldn't particularly mind killing it. As a man who subverted the Constitution and the institutions born of it in order to enhance his own political power, he was of course buried as a hero in Arlington Cemetery with full military honors. Soldiers rode behind his casket on horses, they marched before his casket with guns. On top of his casket was a flag. An American one, I hear. But I don't believe everything I hear.

Cynic then.

I don't have anything more to say now. I have nothing more to say for a while, I think. I was lying in bed this morning wondering if I could get back my job at the comic-book store. I wrote some letters this morning. Dr. Asdrubal Jimenez Vaca, who works for a trade union among the banana plantations of Uraba, Colombia, was shot in an ambush. Karpal Singh is a Malaysian attorney who defends the civil rights of dissidents; he's in an unknown jail for unknown reasons, for an unknown sentence. Three Burmese filmmakers named Thu Ra, Tin Soe and Zin Wyne are being held in prison incommunicado without any reasons given. I have thanked the president of Colombia, the prime minister of Malaysia and the Burmese minister of defense for their attention to these matters.

In the way that every American has his secret America in him, he or she is marked by that secret. In my secret America I once wrote something I should not have. It had a devastating impact on someone's life and vocation. The ramifications of it were such that even now I cannot say anything about it, who it was or when it was or where; for that matter, having just told you that it happened, I must now deny that it happened at all. I occasionally have a dream in which I meet this person, years later, and the fury is still hard in this person's face. Were I to have the opportunity to go back in my life and take back one thing I have done, and though I would certainly have an array of things to choose from, the choice would nonetheless be clear. The alteration or deletion, indeed, of a single word might have changed everything. I thought at the time like all Americans that malice had to lie at the root of evil, that if one was innocent in his intentions he was innocent in his actions. I still haven't decided what it means that no one quite believes I didn't do it on purpose. I don't think you *really* feel guilty about it, someone said to me about a year ago. Driving home I knew he was wrong, but I also knew it didn't matter. I knew he might as well have been right. There's malice, I believe it was said in these pages before, in the naive act that has malicious consequences. And though I cannot say more about it here, you'll just have to take my word for it that what happened and the way it happened has everything to do with America.

A moment ago the phone rang.

It's twilight now, a nice thing to see from this upstairs window. The window faces west to the Hollywood hills and the sun plummets into them in a crash of debauched and then sullen light. The room's magenta. The phone rang. I instantly know that the other end of the line could be anywhere, it has the hush of Anywhere in it. I also know she must take a deep breath before she begins to speak.

• • •

She speaks to me. *I can't live with the things you feel* she says. I have these lapses now but I know this voice. I've heard this voice. We left it behind us somewhere, New Mexico or Arizona. It knocked on my door once, perhaps. *It's enough* she says *to live with the things I feel. It's enough to live with the feeling of the country flowing through me.* She knows I don't have anything more to say now. She knows I have nothing more to say for a while. She's shrewdly chosen this moment, when there's nothing for me to do but say nothing, nothing for me to do but listen. *Don't tell me you ask nothing of me because I hear the unspoken questions in the rush of your breath when I speak to you. You believe in secrets, you talk of them all the time; but that isn't me.* For a moment I take the phone away from my ear as though I'm sure to hear something else.

These days this time of year twilight's only a minute or two. "Wait," I say to the phone. But the voice on the other end wants me out of its life.

I've already gone from it.

I have one secret left.

• • •

I remember this man as soon as I see him. I've been sitting next to him perhaps ten minutes before I happen to look over, but then I remember him right away. There's no mistaking him. Of course I took no notice at first, there's not much to notice but the girls on the runways; what I notice is that he isn't laying his money on the stage. The last girl who danced before us regarded him with scorn, though if she recognized him, she showed no sign of it.

I look over and right away I remember who it is.

It's three nights before the New Year. I'm in a place about five blocks from Los Angeles International Airport. It's insulated from the roar of the airplanes flying overhead, coming in and getting out. The only time you hear them is when someone opens a door to come in or get out. Then the sound of an airplane flies in and crashes against the music. The girls dance to Led Zeppelin, Prince, Guns N' Roses. The disc jockey even plays Bob Marley's "Redemption Song." A woman taking off her clothes to "Redemption Song"? Well, yes, actually. The club is dark and somber, without the festivity of the Cheetah in Atlanta. Four or five girls dance at once, on a runway that extends five different directions into five different islands. The two walls that stretch the length of the room are paneled in mirrors, so at a given moment there may be fifteen pink naked dancers swirling around the room, five of them real and ten of them not. There are also three of you, only one of whom is burdened with the responsibility of actually having to be you. It's a rather quiet party since only a third of the club's population have voices and none of them is much in use. The women dancing don't say anything and the women serving drinks may chat with the men only until they sense an incursion into the riskier realms of familiarity, at which point they move on. The men are quietest of all. It's a male wake, guys attending the memorialization of desires that never flourish and fantasies that never die. By the time they've been there an hour they're lost. The women don't see them and they no longer see the women.

It may be he no longer sees the women. The girl dancing now sees only that he isn't laying his money on the stage. I've put a couple of dollars out, she quietly says thank you when she's finished, picking them up and shooting him a glance. I squirm in my seat a little. I admit it, he's embarrassing me again, like he has before. I remember him walking aimlessly around the outer corridors of the Omni Center at the Democratic Convention, people interested in him for a moment and then losing interest just as quickly. Soon the girls who have danced unrewarded for him will report to the others that there's no percentage in dancing for the tall slightly familiar guy on island four.

"Senator?" It's occurred to me of course that he's been having money problems for some time. I've now pulled my own wad of bills from my shirt pocket and begin to peel a couple off. For a moment he doesn't even acknowledge that someone's spoken to him; then he turns slowly in my direction. "I'm sorry, but . . . you have to give them some money, see."

He looks at me with some alarm. He looks over his shoulder as though he's afraid someone might be watching us. "You talking to me?" he finally asks.

"These women"— I gesture to the empty stage—"they make their living on the tips. It's not right you don't give them something. Look what they've revealed of themselves. These are women without secrets. You have to give them some money." I shrug. "A dollar, even."

I can tell he's embarrassed, perhaps even ashamed. He sighs deeply and turns away again.

"I know you've got some money problems," I go on. I'm making it worse. "You know, I won't say I feel badly for you. I won't say you got a raw deal. We both know that isn't so. We both know you brought it on yourself. I still tend to think you might have made a pretty good president, truth be told. . . ." He looks at me now like I'm out of my mind. "Here." I stick six dollars in his coat pocket. "Just give them each a dollar and it'll at least be something."

With my hand in his coat pocket he about flies out of his chair. He staggers back away from me in the dark; we both look around us to see if people are watching. I can understand it probably appeared a little odd, me sticking my hand in his coat. I throw my hands up as though to show they're empty. "Jesus," he says.

"Sorry, sorry," I start muttering profusely.

"I don't know what you're thinking, pal." He's still looking at the other people in the club, none of whom could care less.

"Sorry."

"If it's not one thing it's another," he says, bitterly angry. He pushes his chair out of the way and brushes past me in a rage. He almost knocks over one of the women serving drinks. I can hear his voice but can no longer make out his words as he makes his way for the exit. The woman serving drinks is coming toward me and I'm thinking she's going to have me thrown out, but then I realize the drink on her tray is one I ordered ten minutes ago. As she reaches me there comes from behind her, but almost as though it comes out of her, an aeronautical scream, the takeoff of a jet overhead just as he's stepping out the door. Beyond her waist I can see him in the doorway almost drop to the ground from the sound of it, covering his head to protect it from the plane hundreds of feet above him. When the waitress sets the drink before me I pay and tip her, it's then I realize he still has my six dollars.

Then you realize you have nothing left of your own. Then you realize you've emptied your pockets now, they're empty for the rest of the night and maybe the rest of the year. Then you realize the girl dancing now before you is going to dance for free because you have nothing to give her, and you're the only one left at this particular island now, you're the only audience she has. She may be the kind of woman who dances only when it's for free, who dances only when you're left and you have nothing left to give her. She's not a complete stranger. She could be any age, she could be any color. She could have been looking for someone and she could have found who she was looking for, and only when she did was she finally free. After only a moment she kicks off her shoes. It's not any sort of flamboyant gesture, she does it more or less at the beginning of things when you barely notice it. Quite unlike every other woman who's danced before you, she shows no sign that she'll entertain either your excesses or deficiencies in whatever fantasy may include them; she was free of that obligation too, when she found who she was looking for. When a guy at a table behind me gets up to leave and puts three dollars on the edge of her stage, she kicks the money off and isn't even aware of having done it. She isn't aware of your homage at all. For some reason it makes it all the more unbearable not to give her something. It makes it all the more unbearable to find nothing in your pockets for her. You rummage your pants, you rummage your shirt. You plunder your wallet. You're reduced to searching your coat pockets for the only thing they have, which is no currency but only, in the last corner, something you don't recognize as yours at all. Something you inherited in one of the lapses of the year that now lies end to end. It's an earring. It's a small silver mask on the end of a small scepter which is stained with something. What does it say to you? What does it tell you beyond your own stutter? In that stutter where the voice of your mind is never quite in sync with the voice of your mouth, what truth do you suppose is whispered? F-F-Fire, it says. Fire in a crowded theater. Fire in an empty strip joint. You can only hope in between the voice of your mind and the voice of your mouth is a country that will be yours again someday. How much easier it would be, to be a man who doesn't love his country. You take the earring and you put it at her bare foot, and you get up to leave quickly because if she kicks it off you don't want to see it. You know at this point she's not dancing in any country but her own. You know that in her own rhythm, with her mouth slightly parted, she might murmur a name, and you know leaving with your back to her that her eyes are still closed and will never see you go. You have this unsettling feeling that this is perilously close to the way she makes love, and whatever name is on her mouth isn't going to be any you recognize. It belongs to someone else. Whoever has caught her eye has already paid to see her dance. He isn't here. He isn't you.